D1521178

Complete Guide to
Football's Option Attacks

Complete Guide to Football's Option Attacks

DREW TALLMAN

PARKER PUBLISHING COMPANY, INC.
West Nyack, N.Y.

© 1977 by

Parker Publishing Company, Inc.

West Nyack, N.Y.

Library of Congress Cataloging in Publication Data

Tallman, Drew.
    Complete guide to football's option attacks.

    Includes index.
    1. Football—Offense. I. Title.
GV951.8.T29   796.33'22   76-56087
ISBN 0-13-160010-9

Printed in the United States of America

Dedicated to

Carl and Betty Rohde

Whose friendship and kindness have benefited so many.

Also by the Author

Directory of Football Defenses: Successful Defenses and How to Attack Them

Football Coach's Guide to a High Scoring Passing Offense

How to Coach Football's Attacking Defenses

Winning Play Sequences in Modern Football

WHAT THIS BOOK OFFERS YOU

This book is a guide to the entire option game. Every option is presented in complete detail. The various and contrasting options included are the wishbone triple option, the veer triple option, swing option, triple and regular outside belly option, isolation option, lead option, cross-buck option, quick pitch option, and the split-T option. Regular and counter options from every series are described and other base plays and counters are also provided. Fundamentals, techniques, and coaching points are clearly illustrated. Every blocking scheme, variation, and adjustment is thoroughly presented. These encompass the most common blocking rules for all options. Different personnel and methods for blocking at the perimeter are shown with or without a backfield fake inside. This embodies a diversity of backs (flankers, slotbacks, wingbacks), tight ends, split ends, guards, and tackles.

Fundamentals and techniques for the quarterback are thoroughly discussed. The actual option techniques, pitching methods, ball control, aiming points, and release are discussed. The importance of the trail back's relationship with the quarterback for the success of the option is also explained. How to play against various defensive end reactions (box, feather, crash, squeeze) and assorted stunts are shown. Triple option techniques (reading and keying the defender inside the defensive end) are completely detailed.

This book provides you with attacking strategies, principles and concepts of an entire option display. It explains how to upset defensive schemes and movements. It includes methods that you and your quarterback can best utilize to take advantage of weaknesses and breakdowns. Practice procedures, plus unique and essential option drills, are also featured.

Championship football offenses realize success because of many factors. Organization, assistants, practice, techniques, drills, conditioning, etc. all play an essential role. However, the style and polish of an offense may be the shade of difference between success and failure. The option game presents more problems to defensive schemes than any other strategy in football. It delivers a piercing blow with finesse, skill, quickness, and speed. This book furnishes insights into every phase of a striking option attack. It will help you become more intelligent, knowledgeable, and strategic with any option game.

Drew Tallman

Acknowledgments

My thanks go to Mrs. Marie Slack for a fine editing job and the typing of the manuscript. I warmly acknowledge the debt due to Matty and Angie Certosimo, who helped so many players who have played the great game of football. And finally a special thanks goes to Sue, Julie, and Holly who love sports and the wonderful outdoors.

CONTENTS

Complete Guide to
Football's Option Attacks

1

TODAY'S OPTION GAMES

The option attack has a significant role in the style of today's football. Not every offense utilizes power alone in attacking defensive front alignments. If a team has a number of quick, big, and strong lineman that can root the defense off the line, then brute force football can easily succeed. However, there are only a few teams in high school and college that can continue to excel with this style of offense.

The option attack relies on the concept and principle of out-maneuvering defensive schemes and personnel by getting the ball to the carrier who is least covered and/or has the most opportunity of gaining yardage. The quarterback is the mainstay of any option attack. He is trained and drilled to read and key defensive movements and quickly react to weaknesses. The dictionary defines option as "the exercise of the power of choice." In this case, the quarterback chooses whether he will deliver or retain the football. He decides the choice, whether it be to himself or one of the other running backs. *Diagram 1-1* illustrates the quarterback advancing along the line of scrimmage and aiming directly at the defensive end. The remaining back follows on a course about four yards in depth and a few yards in front of the

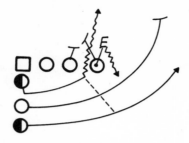

Diagram 1-1

quarterback. The quarterback now has the option to either tuck the football under his arm and turn upfield or pitch to the back. This choice will be determined by the reactions of the defensive end. Fundamentally, if the end attacks the quarterback the ball is automatically delivered. However, if the defensive end collars the halfback the quarterback runs.

CATEGORIZATION OF OPTIONS

There are primarily two categories of options:

1. One choice or option (this involves two people)
2. Two choices or options (this involves three people)

One Option

Allowing the quarterback just one choice is much simpler and easier to execute than perfecting two options. Once the ball is snapped, a faking backfield scheme may be accomplished in the interval. The quarterback goes directly to the defensive man he is to option. The defender to option includes almost any man since there are many and various option attacks, formations, and defensive adjustments. The option can also occur anywhere along the line of scrimmage or upfield into the defensive secondary areas. *Diagram 1-2* indicates one option. In this case, the quarterback reads the reactions of the defensive tackle while placing the ball into the stomach of the fullback. The quarterback automatically shifts his eyes to the defensive tackle once the ball is snapped. If the tackle remains in his original alignment or charges out and away from the fullback, the ball is naturally given to him. If,

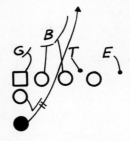

The defensive tackle reacts out so the ball is handed to the fullback.

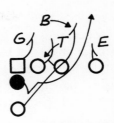

The defensive tackle slants inside. The offensive tackle picks him up on his charge. The fullback veers outside for the linebacker with the quarterback following directly behind him.

Diagram 1-2

however, the defender slants toward the dive, the quarterback removes the ball from the stomach and follows the fullback upfield for yardage. The blocking along the line is basically one on one except the offensive tackle blocks inside as shown. The fullback attempts to block any defenders pursuing outside.

Another clear example is shown in *Diagram 1-3*. In this instance, however, the ball is brought to the defensive cornerback aligned out-

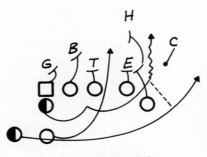

Diagram 1-3

side the offensive wingback. The fake of the fullback is initiated at the off-tackle area. A double team or a seal type of block is executed by the wingback on the defensive end or linebacker. Once the quarterback completes the fake, he withdraws the ball from the fullback and sprints outside the double team block. He scans immediately for the defensive corner. If the corner attacks the quarterback, he pitches to his halfback. If, however, the corner covers the halfback, the quarterback tucks the ball away and sprints for as much yardage as he can achieve.

Two Options (The Triple Option)

Two option choice is more difficult for the quarterback to master. An extensive amount of time, drilling, and training is necessary in order for the quarterback to become proficient. There are various examples of the two option attack (known as the triple option because of the ability of three offensive backs having the opportunity, during the execution of the play, to receive the football). With this mode of attack, there occurs no other faking. Therefore, the quarterback read is realized immediately. The quarterback takes the ball from center and places it to the back driving into the line. (In any two option attack, the play always begins with a halfback or fullback diving towards the line of scrimmage.) At the same time the quarterback glances at the defender, he is responsible to key *(Diagram 1-4)*. If the defender closes for the back the quarterback keeps the ball himself and sprints directly toward his next read. If the defensive man does not attack, the halfback automatically receives the football. Once the quarterback, however, realizes he must hold the ball, he continues to the next defender and reacts to his movements (pitch or keep).

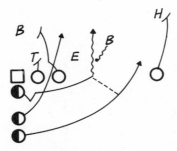

The Two Option Choice (The Triple Option)

Diagram 1-4

OPTION AREAS

Since there are a wide variety of plays and series, various option areas along the line of scrimmage result. *Diagram 1-5* illustrates the three running areas that options can attack. The first option area is located from the center to the outside shoulder of the offensive tackle. In area 1, a fullback or halfback must be utilized to drive toward the line of scrimmage in anticipation of receiving the football. Whether he receives the ball or not is dependent upon the reactions of an interior lineman aligned and reacting to the play. At the same instant, the quarterback is receiving the ball from the center and shifting his eyes to that defender. The quarterback places the ball into the stomach of the offensive back and keys, reads, and executes according to the defensive reaction. The regular option or first part of the triple option play can begin at area 1.

Area 2 is the most often attacked, since most option plays are brought to the defensive end located there. Most regular options (one choice) go to this area, with the triple option either starting or finishing at this point.

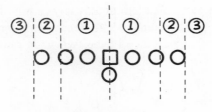

Diagram 1-5

Area 3 is the least attacked area for the running option game. Some regular and triple option plays will extend into area three. All options in this zone are directed to defensive secondary personnel. The quarterback is usually maneuvering upfield since he is now outside the defensive contain man.

OPTIONS AND PLAY SEQUENCES

There are many series from which options can be executed. Some require fakes up the middle with the quarterback moving along the line of scrimmage to the defensive end. Others require fakes near the off-tackle hole with the option directed outside to the defensive secondary.

Still other options can occur from counter plays or sequences that begin one way, but actually attack in the opposite direction. No matter the style of attack a team utilizes, therefore, different and various option plays can be performed.

FORMATIONS AND OPTIONS

Attacking defenses with the correct formation is important. Closed and tight sets may be more effective against varying defensive alignments than open formations would be. Wide-out formations on one or both sides may be a determining factor to the success of any option play, also. One clear example is the outside triple option sequence. It is, at times, more advantageous to utilize a tight end versus a nine-man front defense (5-4, Pro-4, 4-3, 5-4 Stack, etc.) than an eight-man front (4-4, Wide-Tackle 6, Gap-6, etc.). *Diagram 1-6* illustrates this point. The outside veer triple option receives an appropriate double team against the nine-man front with the potential ball carrier veering toward the off-tackle position. The quarterback is keying the end. However, versus an eight-man defensive front the tight end must block alone with no assistance coming from the offensive tackle. Therefore, versus this look, it is advisable to split an end or set two wide receivers to a side. This eliminates any required blocking at the off-tackle hole. In most instances it forces a defender to align off the line for pass coverage assistance of the two wide-outs.

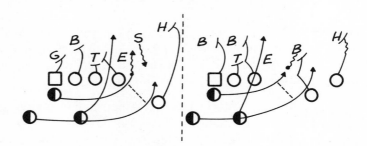

Diagram 1-6

A double team is initiated at the left portion of the diagram with the quarterback keying the defensive end. A one-on-one block by the offensive end is not necessary when setting a formation as shown on the right side of the diagram

Other formations can dictate and control defensive alignments and coverages for the offensive option game. It may require the offense to split the opposite or backside end in order to slow defensive secondary rotation. In many cases a three-deep secondary may not even be able to rotate. Motion and/or shifting may assist the option to create better blocking angles and/or attack defensive alignments easier.

SERIES AND THE OPTION GAME

As previously mentioned, an option attack can be used with almost any series. Some series, of course, are strictly geared towards an option attack. The formations are essentially kept similar. The quarterback and the entire team consistently strive and drill on the primary option attack. No other series is employed. A number of coaches believe success is only derived through consistent execution and drilling of that particular option series. The wishbone and veer attacks are two obvious examples. Yet, there are other coaches and teams that install two or three series, but still utilize the main ingredient of an option attack. There are other offenses, however, which are multiple, that utilize five to six running series, but still realize effective option games. The philosophy of the coach is what determines the style of offense and the number of options to be employed. Whatever is accomplished though, the option game is usually necessary for success of any offensive unit. Speed, techniques, fundamentals, skills, timing, and formations all play an essential role and should be worked upon daily.

Following are the various play sequences in which the option game plays a significant and necessary part. As can be seen from some series, the option is a total attack. Others, however, utilize an option play within the series.

The Swing Option *(Diagram 1-7)*

> *Type of Option:* It is a regular option with the quarterback sprinting directly along the line at the defensive end.
>
> *Purpose:* To attack the defensive outside perimeter as fast and as quickly as possible. Speed is the key. The defensive end must react quickly and the quarterback should converge on him immediately.
>
> *Style of Attack:* The swing option can be executed from any

sequence the offense administers. It is the simpliest of options to coordinate between the line, quarterback, and backfield.

Formations: While it can be executed from any backfield alignment (motion or regular halfback position), it is most successful from the "I" formation.

Advantages: Attacks quickly at the defensive end and outside perimeter. The defense must have good pursuit speed.

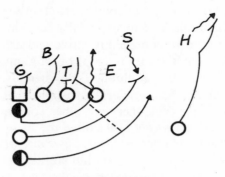

Diagram 1-7

The Split-Veer Option *(Diagram 1-8)*

Type of Option: It can either be a regular or triple option play. A quick dive is initiated inside the tackle before the quarterback proceeds to the defensive end. The outside triple option can be executed from the series, also.

Purpose: To drive inside quickly with a fast halfback. If the ball is not handed to the halfback, the quarterback automatically approaches the defensive end.

Style of Attack: This is a wide formation offense. It is a quick-hitting running game in coordination with a passing attack.

Formations: Wide-out receivers are necessary to spread the defense. Halfbacks are utilized first as runners and then receivers. If the defense aligns tight for the run, the offense expects to pass the ball. If the defense covers wide, the offense should run.

Advantages: It forces the defense to play a quick-hitting forward attack. The defense not only reacts to an option game, but must prepare to cover the pass as well.

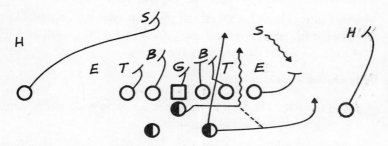

The Inside Veer Triple Option

Diagram 1-8

The Wishbone Option *(Diagram 1-9)*

Type of Option: It is primarily an inside triple option. However, the regular option or outside triple option can be executed.

Purpose: To attack the defense with quickness and power.

Style of Attack: It is only a running offense. Little passing is employed. Power strategy and running is the rule.

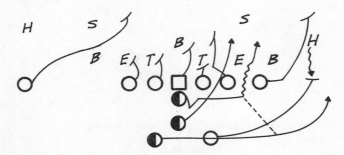

The Wishbone Option Attack

Diagram 1-9

Formations: A three-back backfield in the form of a wishbone is usually utilized. The halfbacks are used as runners and blockers. Other formations both tight (the T formation) and wide (a flanker-split end combination) can be used. A power designed offense is removed when the flanker set is applied.

Advantages: Three backs are aligned for running and blocking. Finesse (the triple option) and power (the ability of three backs to block) is the mainstay of the attack.

The Belly Option *(Diagram 1-10)*

Type of Option: The Belly can either be a triple option as shown or employed as a regular option.

Purpose: To attack the off-tackle hole with finesse. It can also attack the defensive perimeter.

Style of Attack: It can be used with any offensive game.

Formations: Any number of formations can be utilized. Both wide-out and tight sets have been successful.

Advantages: The fullback can roll the belly back inside although it is geared to go off-tackle. Triple option finesse is the key. The perimeter is attacked with the option game also.

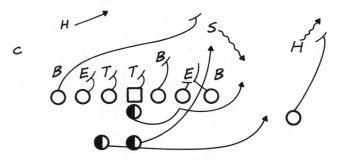

The Outside Triple Belly Option

Diagram 1-10

The Halfback Roll (Lead) Option *(Diagram 1-11)*

Type of Option: The halfback roll can either be a regular option attacking the defensive corner or designed as a triple option.

Purpose: To attack the off-tackle hole from the "I" tailback position. The roll is a "run to daylight" play where the half-back receives the football deep in the backfield and has the opportunity to "roll" inside or outside, according to where the open areas occur.

Style of Attack: Three offensive backs are necessary for execution of the play. The option can be utilized with any offensive game. It is excellent when the halfback possesses speed and the knack of locating the open areas in the defense.

Formations: An "I" formation must be used and the remaining back aligned in a position to receive the pitch.

Advantages: The ability to execute an option from a good off-tackle power play.

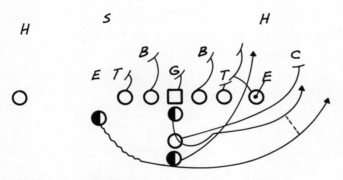

The Halfback Roll (Lead) Triple Option

Diagram 1-11

The Isolation Option *(Diagram 1-12)*

Type of Option: It is regular option at the defensive end.

Purpose: To attack a defensive end after a good fake has been completed inside.

Style of Attack: Any offense can exploit it. The isolation series from the "I" tailback's position should occur often.

Formations: It must be executed from the "I" formation with the remaining back in an alignment to receive the pitch from the quarterback.

Advantages: The option is excellent when the primary inside isolation play is successful or the defense is inside conscious in attempting to halt it.

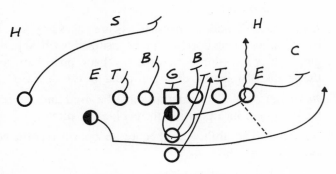

The Isolation Option

Diagram 1-12

The Split-T Option *(Diagram 1-13)*

Type of Option: It is regular option at the defensive end with a fake by a ball carrier inside.

Purpose: To split the defense and hit areas along the line of scrimmage quickly with diving halfbacks.

Style of Attack: The split-T is a running offense first with little passing. Splitting the defense is important, with the ability to dive halfbacks quickly. It is a power style of offense, also.

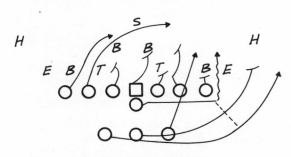

The Split-T Option

Diagram 1-13

Formations: The ''T'' formation. Splitting of an end can be accomplished also.

Advantages: Splitting the defense and attacking quickly along the line.

The Cross-Buck Option *(Diagram 1-14)*

Type of Option: It is regular option play.

Purpose: To freeze linebackers, as well as other personnel inside, so the quarterback or halfback has the opportunity to run off-tackle or outside.

Style of Attack: It is an excellent play from the Delaware Wing-T. It can be deployed with any cross-buck action in the backfield.

Formations: Any formation where cross-buck action can be used (the I, normal halfback position, or starting back towards the center in motion). The remaining halfback can be stationed anywhere.

Advantages: It freezes defenders inside, especially when the faking back has had success driving in the opposite direction.

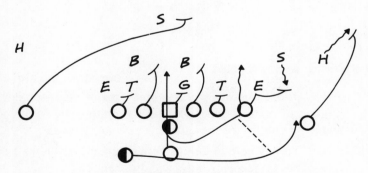

The Cross-Buck Regular Option

Diagram 1-14

The Quick Pitch Option *(Diagram 1-15)*

Type of Option: A regular option play designed from the fake of the quick pitch.

Purpose: To attack the defensive end's reactions. If the end continually widens, due to the quick pitch, the quarterback can execute the option and run inside. Once the end closes for the quarterback, the quick pitch or option pitch can be effective.

Style of Attack: Any offense can easily use the option from the quick pitch.

Formations: Good versus a wide-out set. The halfback must be aligned in his regular position.

Advantages: It is valuable to counteract the defense end's movements to the quick pitch.

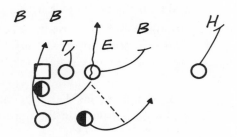

The Quick Pitch Option

Diagram 1-15

Option Passing from Dropback *(Diagram 1-16)*

Type of Option: Various key and read options are essential. The number of options depends upon the philosophy of the coach and/or the ability of the quarterback and receivers.

Purpose: To key certain defensive movements so the ball is delivered to the receiver most widely open.

Style of Attack: Usually a pro-type offensive attack. A great deal of passing is employed.

Formations: Usually two receivers are spread to one or both sides (flanker-split end or twins set).

Advantages: To strategically out-maneuver the defense on every pass thrown. If the defense reacts one way, the ball is thrown in the opposite direction, etc.

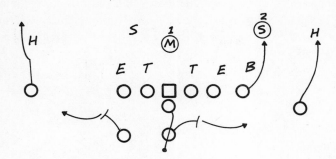

The Drop-back Pass

Diagram 1-16

Option Passing from Sprint-Out *(Diagram 1-17)*

Type of Option: Passing to the receiver least encountered according to the reactions and coverages of the defense.

Purpose: To form different passing lanes, roll-away from the defense rush, read the open receiver, and/or get outside.

Style of Attack: Any offense can be applied with the sprint-out series.

Formations: Any formation can be utilized.

Advantages: To strategically out-maneuver and react away from the defensive secondary coverage with sound pass patterns.

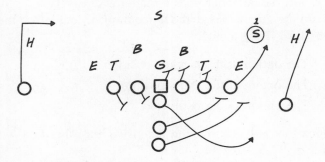

The Sprint-out Option Passing Game

Diagram 1-17

2

THE OPTION QUARTERBACK

While there is an array of options that includes the inside and outside triple options and regular options at the defensive tackle, end, and perimeter areas, the actual option technique remains similar. Whether a fake is initiated inside, a counter action is demonstrated, or the quarterback moves directly along the line of scrimmage, the actual option versus the defender does not alter extensively.

There are three areas, already mentioned, that attack the defense along the line. They include:

1. The option at the tackle's position
2. The option at the end's position
3. The option at the perimeter

Since most options occur at the defensive end, this first will be explained and illustrated.

OPTIONING THE DEFENSIVE END

There are many ways the quarterback can attack the defensive end. Different angles or courses are involved, also. The defensive end can be attacked with the outside triple option or with the regular option. Here the pitch or run is attained according to the movements of the defensive end.

THE REGULAR OPTION AT THE DEFENSIVE END

The quarterback can bring the ball to the end with or without a fake inside. Various fakes can include the fullback, tailbacks, counter movements, etc. No matter the execution, the quarterback steps around each fake and aims at the defensive end. *Diagram 2-1* illustrates the various paths in which the quarterback can travel when attacking the defender. As can be seen, the movement at the end can be straight along the line or can arrive at various angles.

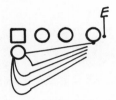

Diagram 2-1

The path designed for the quarterback is important. It is first essential the quarterback advance into the line as far as possible. This, of course, will vary due to the blocks executed by the offensive end and tackle. As long as the quarterback can proceed into the line, the extra yardage can be achieved if he holds onto the ball and a preferable pitching relationship with the trailing halfback occurs.

Another fundamental aspect of the option path is the quarterback's angle toward the line. While some options are designed to move directly along the line, it is advantageous if the quarterback can have an angle into it. *Diagram 2-1* illustrates various angles a quarterback can be directed on different plays. The further the quarterback is away from the line before aiming toward the defensive end, the better opportunity he has to turn upfield and run. By sprinting along the line of scrimmage, the quarterback's shoulders are perpendicular to the line of scrimmage. When he is ready to pitch the football, he must turn his shoulders slightly since the pitch halfback should be slightly ahead of him. From this position the quarterback cannot see any defenders inside or opposite him on the line. When he decides to run with the football, he must turn at approximately 90 degrees and then react to the running lanes. If the option is designed for the quarterback to maneuver along the line, the quarterback should be taught to advance into it as far as possible, so he is attacking the defensive end at a better angle.

Irregular Paths

It is essential the quarterback attack the end correctly. Two of the biggest mistakes executed by quarterbacks are charging the end by circling him or moving away from the line of scrimmage *(Diagram 2-2)*. A circling effect causes the quarterback precious seconds. Speed is the essence in any option. Running an extended path results in a slower time and allows the defense to control the option. It also disrupts the timing between the quarterback and the pitch man. Additional problems are created by moving away from the line of scrimmage. If the quarterback decided to run it would take him longer just to get back to the line of scrimmage. Of course, this allows the defense time to catch him. Secondly, there is absolutely no pitch relationship with the halfback. The defensive end should be able to cover both possible ball carriers with ease.

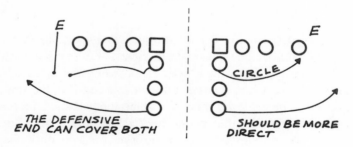

Diagram 2-2

Optional Techniques at the Defensive End

The first important ingredient of the option is *speed*. The quarterback must attack the defensive end as quickly and as fast as possible whether a fake is initiated or not. While time is of the split second, it can result in the success of the play. If the quarterback can advance to the defensive end before any pursuing defenders, long yardage can be achieved. If an offense utilizes the option to a sizable extent it is essential that speed be drilled daily. Speed and quickness can easily be developed and achieved, but only through continuous work and practice time. Off-season conditioning with the quarterbacks and backfield should be worked at, also.

Two Pitching Methods

There are actually two pitching methods when attacking the defensive end. Each has its merits and advantages. They include:

1. The Overhand Flip
2. The Quick Toss

The Overhand Flip Option Technique

If the quarterback has completed any fake into the line, he immediately brings the ball up to chest level with two hands. As he quickly dashes along the line of scrimmage, the ball must remain at the level described. This is known as the *ready* position. He is automatically prepared to pitch the ball quickly should any quick force be made by the defensive end. The end *will not* always be waiting on the line of scrimmage for the quarterback to drive at him. The end may be on a forceful stunt inside attempting to tackle the quarterback before he has the opportunity to pitch the ball. He must control the ball at the ready position at all times.

Ball Control

The ball is firmly held with the hand farthest from the line of scrimmage. This is the hand and arm that flips the ball to the trailing back. *Photo 2-1* indicates the quarterback's hand placement near the chest level. Usually the fingers are grasping the laces by the middle of the ball. The palm of the hand rests on the remaining portion of the ball. The point of the ball is pointing upward. The other hand is used only to help secure the ball. If for any reason the quarterback is knocked or forced off balance, he should be able to protect the ball and not fumble.

As the quarterback is running along the line, the elbows remain near the body in a natural running movement. The ball is shuttled back and forth across the chest in coordination with the running movement. Any unnatural movement should be corrected. There are a multitude of

other techniques that have to be drilled, so that the coach cannot afford to be distracted by this problem. As long as the ball is held firmly with the flipping hand, with the quarterback in full control of the ball, the option is at a good embarkment.

Aiming Point and Shoulder Position

As long as the defensive end remains on or near the line of scrimmage, the quarterback should aim for his inside shoulder. Reading the inside shoulder is helpful. If the end lunges for the quarterback, the shoulder area will automatically appear. It also enables the quarterback to aim at an inside approach down the line. The shoulders should be turned slightly towards the neutral zone. Of course the angle at which the quarterback is directed will be determined by the faking action, if any, in the backfield. The shoulders should be turned considerably towards the line. The quarterback has a better opportunity to turn upfield if he decides to carry the ball. The offensive halfback should be well in front of the quarterback's outside hip, so when the ball is flipped, it will be forward.

Approach and Body Control

As mentioned previously, speed is essential for the success of any option. However, there is a point when the quarterback must decelerate and control this speed as he approaches the defensive end. The slowing process begins approximately 2½-3 yards from the defensive end. As the quarterback arrives at this point, he immediately lowers his center of gravity, shortens his stride to quick steps, and concentrates on the reactions of the end. His eyes never glance away from his aiming point. He has distance of approximately 1½-2 yards to halt his progression at the defensive end and read his reactions. He should arrive and be a ½ yard from the defensive end, moving his feet quickly, and within a fraction of time decide whether to keep or toss the football. At this meeting, the head is up, ball in a good ready position, hips are down, knees are bent (to push and run), and feet flowing quickly.

Ball Release and Control of the Defensive End

As the quarterback halts his forward progression, a quick decision must be forthcoming. It is based strictly on the movements of the end. No guesswork is involved. Drilling the various movements of the defensive end should eliminate any mistakes. The fundamental pitch to the offensive halfback or receiver is the *overhand flip*. This is achieved rather easily. The overhand pitch can be executed by two means. One is the *quick* and vigorous release. This propels the ball to the receiver quickly. Percentage-wise, however, there is a likelihood of the ball going astray or the halfback dropping the ball. The second method is the *soft* release. Again the flip is overhand, but it is executed softly and with a slight arc to the delivery. This results in an easier catch for the receiver. If the ball happens to go behind or is thrown in a haphazard manner, the receiver has a better opportunity to catch it.

The Quick Release

When the quarterback decides to release the ball because of the defensive end's reactions, the arm should be vigorously pushed out and away from the body. The ball is moved across the chest approximately six inches. The off hand (not pitching the ball) is a guiding hand with the palm aiming directly to the receiver. This naturally turns the shoulders slightly toward the pitch man. The head is a swivel and turns quickly with the shoulders and hands towards the trailing back. It becomes, in a matter of a split second, an eye and hand coordinating feat with the flip of the ball.

It is now the responsibility of the pitch arm to aim and throw the ball with accuracy. As the ball leaves the guide hand, the pitch hand has full control of the football for a range of approximately a foot. This is not difficult. The palm rises slightly up, with the fingers grasping the football so it will not fall. The wrist turns the hand so the palm begins to face in the direction of the pitch. At the same instant, the body pushes off the opposite foot and leans slightly toward the receiver. The opposite leg is placed forward for balance. The elbow and upper arm extend from the body, and the forearm begins to straighten as the flip occurs. The wrist continues to rotate toward the trailback and begins to propel the ball forcefully toward the receiver. This entire action is natural and aggressive and is completed within a second of time. *Photo 2-2* illustrates the quarterback's and halfback's relationship for the option pitch.

The Soft Release

The soft release is executed in the exact manner described. The only difference is the quarterback's forceful release. All he needs to accomplish is to aim the ball at the receiver and release it with less acceleration. The ball should have a slight arc so the ball carrier can easily grab it.

The Shoulder Dip Technique

Another method utilized by a few coaches is the shoulder dip technique. Its purpose is an attempt to force the defensive end to react inward to him. As the defensive end does so, the quarterback quickly pitches the ball. The quarterback attacks the defender in the same manner described previously. However, as he slows his progression, he pushes with his outside foot and slightly turns upfield into the neutral zone. He *does not* turn his shoulders. As the defensive end reacts inside, the quarterback merely pitches the ball. It should be clearly understood that the ball is being flipped while the quarterback is thrusting in the opposite direction. The body lean is into the line. All the force generated is with the arm, wrist, and hand.

The Quick Toss

Another effective pitching motion is the quick-toss technique. There are numerous teams that employ it and for good reasons. Teams that utilize it are usually the wishbone and split-veer offenses. The pitch is driven from the hip and thrust quickly in an opposite side-arm fashion known in baseball.

The single factor most offenses prefer is that the actual ball handling and faking to driving backs into the line is executed low and near the hips. Since most defenses attempt to stunt and disrupt the triple and regular options of these offenses, the quarterback must be completely prepared to deliver the ball immediately to the pitch man. Throwing from the hip eliminates bringing the ball to chest level and pitching it. This creates time which otherwise is necessary to pitch. Another reason is its forcefulness. The ball is thrust out quickly and with speed. A slight disadvantage is the practice and drill work required. It is slightly more difficult to learn. However, once it is executed a number of times and drilled upon daily, many mistakes are eliminated.

The Approach and Body Control

Speed, again, is essential once all faking is completed. However, the body remains slightly crouched as it approaches the defensive end. The hips are lower, but similar quick and short aggressive steps are used when arriving at the pitch intersection. The aiming point and shoulder position remain the same.

Ball Control

The ball is held with two hands. One is a grasping hand while the other is used for guiding. The fingers grip the ball higher, but surround the laces. The release of the ball is uniquely different from the overhand. A firmer control of the ball with the hands is essential also. It is set lower than the belt-buckle. The ball is at a 45 degree angle to the ground. Both wrists are cocked for deliverance. The ball is shuttled back and forth across the belt-line in short-quick movements which coordinate with the running.

The Release

The release is initiated with the flip or pitch hand in firm control of the ball. In this case, the wrist rotates downward so the thumb points toward the ground. The elbow and upper arm leave the body, and the forearm begins to straighten. The wrist and thumb continue to rotate downward and away toward the pitch man *(Photo 2-3)*. The palm faces the ground. The ball is propelled with the assistance of the middle finger and forefinger as the hand turns completely as far as it can rotate. It is a quick and forceful action, with the ball released and caught by the trail back in a matter of a split second.

Irregular Methods

There are other styles in which the ball can be pitched to the receiver. Usually these are haphazard methods that do not require much teaching or skill. The quarterback does what comes naturally to him. One technique is to pitch the ball with two hands. This materializes when the quarterback doesn't have confidence in the release mechanism of his pitch arm. It is similar to a basketball pass. A second method is utilizing the opposite hand for the pitch. The arm and hand farthest from the trail back expels the ball across the body and toward the halfback. This occurs because, again, the quarterback does not have enough faith in the proper flip arm.

THE HALFBACK'S (RECEIVER'S) RELATIONSHIP WITH THE QUARTERBACK

The pitch back's relationship with the quarterback is important for the success of the option. It is essential he arrive at a point where he achieves the same relationship with the quarterback every instant. No matter the various options executed, whether it be a dive, counter fake, or no dive at all, the back's responsibility is to remain in the proper pitch relationship.

Diagram 2-3 indicates the relationship of the quarterback and pitch man. The trail back's bearing to the quarterback is approximately four yards in depth and three yards outside him and the defensive end. His footwork and speed are essential to arrive at and maintain this position. False steps cannot occur. This is a good spot, because as the ball is released, it is virtually impossible for the defensive end to cover the

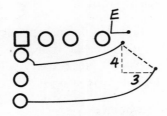

Diagram 2-3

The halfback is 4 yards in depth and 3 yards out-side the quarterback and defensive end.

pitch man as well. The pitch back is also outside and at the perimeter starting toward the line of scrimmage. If the quarterback decides to turn upfield, the halfback should immediately swing with the quarterback. The halfback strives to remain behind the quarterback in case he decides to pitch downfield.

Diagram 2-4 illustrates two abnormal pitch relationships. If the pitch receiver is directly behind, even though the depth is correct, the defensive end has the ability and position to recover from the quarterback and pursue along the line to the halfback. The other possibility occurs when the receiver widens too far outside the defensive end. In this case, the end has the opportunity to block the pitch. Since the ball must be led out in front of the halfback it is a difficult pitch to deliver.

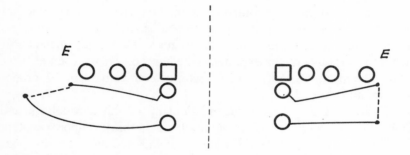

Pitch back is too far removed from the pitch point.

Halfback does not have enough width.

Diagram 2-4

DEFENSIVE END PLAY

There are many actions the defense and defensive end can try to stop any option. The quarterback, therefore, must be thoroughly trained, drilled, and prepared to meet every situation that arises. The various reactions of the defensive end include:

1. The Feather Technique
2. The Box Technique
3. The Crash Technique
4. The Squeeze Technique

The Feather Technique

This is usually the first reaction taught a defensive end to play the option. He learns to remain on the line of scrimmage, keep the shoulders parallel to the line., and position the outside leg out and behind the inside one *(Diagram 2-5)*. As the quarterback approaches the feather (sometimes referred to as the cat and mouse technique), he should attack the inside shoulder of the defender as quickly as possible and force him to make a decision. If the end continues to retreat, attempting to play both the quarterback and the pitch, the quarterback should have enough area to swerve inside and run. Once he diverts upfield, he immediately attempts to get outside again to stay away from any pursuit inside. If, however, the defensive end reacts toward the quarterback, he automatically pitches the ball. The defender should never be able to cover the trailing halfback.

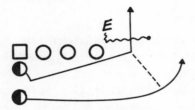

The Cat and Mouse or Feather Technique

Diagram 2-5

The Box Technique

There are different schemes defensive players are taught when the box technique is applied. Some are required to cross the line approximately 1½ yards and hold that position for containment purposes. If this is the case, the quarterback aims inside and reacts from the defenders' movements. If the end attacks the quarterback,the pitch should be well off and away. If the defender reacts to the pitch halfback, the quarterback should keep and run with the football *Diagram 2-6)*.

A defensive end can penetrate the same distance, but turns his shoulders in toward the quarterback. His shoulders and body are now perpendicular to the line. If this is the case, the quarterback immediately tosses the ball to his receiver. The defender should never be able to turn and catch the trailing back.

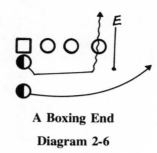

A Boxing End

Diagram 2-6

Other boxing ends may go deeper into the backfield. If this occurs, the quarterback automatically dips upfield and runs. If the defender does penetrate a good distance, the quarterback should be prepared for any inside stunt from the perimeter defenders.

The Crash Technique

The tactic of the crash by a defender is the easiest for the quarterback to spot. A quick decision is already established for him. The ball is pitched immediately. However, preparation is essential for the quarterback. Since the ball is tossed quickly, the quarterback must secure the ball in the ready position even though fakes may occur in the backfield. *Diagram 2-7* illustrates the crash technique.

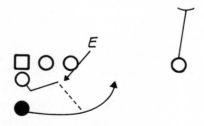

The Crash Technique

Diagram 2-7

The Squeeze Technique

The squeeze technique is an attempt by the defender to drift from the quarterback as if he is responsible for the pitch. At the last instant, however, he squeezes the quarterback for the run. Again the quarterback must react according to the position he attains with the end. If the defender is dropping away, the quarterback can run the ball. If the defender attacks, the quarterback can decide immediately as long as he drives to the end with speed and reacts quickly *(Diagram 2-8)*.

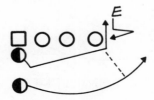

The Squeeze Technique

Diagram 2-8

READING STUNTS

The quarterback will be involved with various blitzes at the perimeter. If the offense is option oriented, the quarterback will see a multiple of stunts. In most cases, the quarterback options the end defender on the line of scrimmage. The offensive line aims to seal the defenders inside the tackle's position. If a stunt occurs, it will be outside the offensive tackle. The quarterback must be unequivocally trained and drilled to react to stunting that causes various defensive alterations. Chapter 3 details how to train and prepare the quarterback to read stunts and perimeter fires.

If the quarterback pitches or keeps from the actions of another defender, he reads this as he travels down the line. Blocking on the corner must be coordinated, also. The blocker assigned to the outside defender may now have to block the defensive end. Blocking patterns and various stunts are thoroughly discussed in Chapter 4.

Diagram 2-9 illustrates a stunt developing at the corner. The outside defensive invert pressures inside the end. The defensive tackle scoops inside while the end protects outside. The quarterback must read this and decide whether to run or pitch from the invert defender. The invert safety may be so aggressive that he may whip past the quarterback. However, he may force a quick play at the quarterback and, therefore, the ball will be pitched. The defensive end must now be picked up according to the blocking scheme employed.

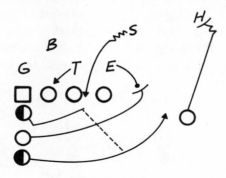

Diagram 2-9

OPTIONING THE DEFENDER INSIDE THE END

The quarterback also reacts on certain options to read the movements of the defender located inside the defensive end's alignment. The seven-man front teams usually align a defender opposite the offensive tackle. The eight-man fronts set defenders over or slightly inside the offensive end. In either case, the quarterback keys these defenders according to the play called. The halfback or fullback utilized in the play read and key this defender also.

There are two classification of plays that read and key the inside defender.

1. The quarterback's read to either hand-off or run.
2. The quarterback's read to either give, or continue toward the next option (Triple option).

Hand-off or Run

The assignment of the fullback or halfback (depending upon the series applied) is explained in detail in the following chapters. However, at the snap of the ball, the quarterback focuses his eyes on the inside defender. The diving back explodes from his stance and aims for the guard-tackle seam. The quarterback doesn't present the ball to the back if the defender slants inside. The back reads this also and blocks him. The quarterback secures the ball and turns to run upfield. The defensive end is blocked by the offensive end *(Diagram 2-10)*. If the defender stays or loops outside, the ball is handed to the dive back.

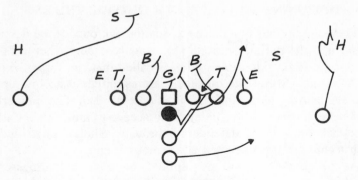

Diagram 2-10

The Triple Option

Reading the inside defender can be realized by two means. The quarterback can slide along the line and hand the ball to the diving back if the defender stays or loops-out *(Diagram 2-11)*. If he slants inside, the quarterback holds the ball and continues to the next option *(Diagram 2-12)*. However, the quarterback can be taught to read this differently. In this instance, if the inside defender slants inside or stays normal, the quarterback does not hand-off the ball. The back now blocks the defender. Only when the defensive man loops outside does the quarterback deliver the ball.

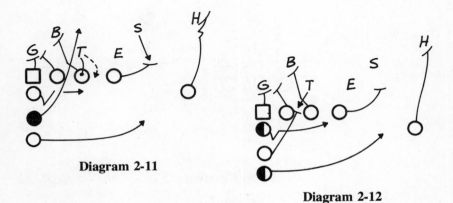

Diagram 2-11

Diagram 2-12

OPTIONING THE DEFENDER OUTSIDE THE END

There are options that place the quarterback outside the defensive end and into the perimeter area. This usually occurs when a fake is off-tackle or an outside triple option is called that can force the quarterback outside. Speed and quickness are essential. Wheeling upfield and not extending along the line is important also. The quarterback should never hesitate for the defender to accede to him. In contrast, he must attack the outside defender vigorously. Similar pitch and approach techniques are executed at a defensive end.

As the quarterback swerves upfield, he reads the various coverages. If an invert coverage materializes from a four deep, he must be prepared to either pitch or run quickly. However, if it is a corner rotation to a flanker set, all the quarterback needs to do is veer upfield and run. *Diagrams 2-13* and *2-14* illustrate these coverages. Reading coverages is not difficult. The quarterback focuses his eyes on the inside defender. If he flows forward or delays, the quarterback options him. If the secondary defender scrambles backward or drives to the deep one-third of the field, the quarterback keeps the football.

It is essential the faking back block or seal off pursuit from the inside if he does not receive the football. This assists the quarterback when he turns upfield to option. It is also the responsibility of the pitch halfback to remain outside the quarterback approximately four yards. If the quarterback decides at any time to pitch, he must be in position to catch the ball.

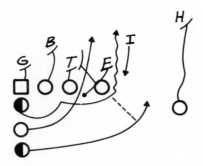

Invert Coverage

Diagram 2-13

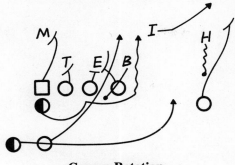

Corner Rotation

Diagram 2-14

3

QUARTERBACK OPTION STRATEGY

Mental conditioning of the quarterback is as important as the physical preparation. He must acquire a thorough knowledge and complete understanding of defenses, their structure, and their stunt, slant, and blitz capabilities. An integrated comprehension of the theory and concepts of defenses, along with the techniques and responsibilities of the positions, should be understood. He also must understand the offense's blocking schemes, backfield maneuvers, and methods of attacking the defense. This chapter deals with the mental preparation of the quarterback. By understanding and mastering defenses and the various responsibilities defenders have on the option, the offense will be more deliberate and effective.

DEFENSIVE STRUCTURE

There are three general catagories of defenses. They include:

1. The Seven-Man Front Defenses

2. The Eight-Man Front Defenses

3. The Unbalanced Defense

The Seven-Man Front Defenses

The seven-man front defenses (an example is shown in *Diagram 3-1*) consist of the 5-4 Oklahoma, Pro-4, variations of the 4-3, Gap-Stack, etc. The alignment characteristics of these defenses are the following:

1. It is a Seven-Man Front—Seven defensive linemen and linebackers in any combination design the forcing unit.

2. It is a 4-Deep secondary—Four perimeter defenders are utilized for the pass. Various coverages are installed for both the pass and the option game.

3. It consists of a one-on-one relationship—A single defender is responsible for one offensive man and/or area.

4. It is a balanced defense—There are the same amount of defenders on both sides of the center.

5. There are five defenders located inside for the offensive running game (a line is drawn through the outside shoulder of the tackle). These defenders are responsible for the inside runners of any option attack.

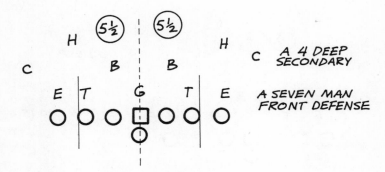

Diagram 3-1

The 5-4 Oklahoma Defense is an example of a seven-man front and four deep defense. It is balanced with "5½" defenders on either side of the center.

6. There are two men (defensive ends) aligned outside the tackles—They are responsible for the quarterback on any option.

7. The cornerbacks or safeties are assigned to the pitch-back.

The Eight-Man Front Defenses

The eight-man front defenses *(Diagram 3-2)* consist of the Split-6, Split 4-4, Wide Tackle-6, 5-3 Gap, 5-3 Wide, etc. The alignment characteristics of these defenses are as follows:

1. It is an eight-man front—Eight defenders are on or near the line of scrimmage (Any combination of linemen and linebackers) and are considered the forcing unit.

2. It is a 3-deep secondary—Three defenders are fundamentally responsible for the pass. They are usually not involved with responsibilities of the option game as with the four spoke.

3. It is designed as a "Gap" responsible defense—Since eight gaps exist (7 offensive linemen), defenders are either aligned into or responsible for these seams.

4. It is a balanced defense—There are the same amount of defenders on both sides of the center.

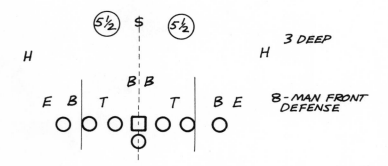

Diagram 3-2

The Split 4-4 Defense is an example of the eight-man front. It is a balanced defense with four defenders inside for the running game and four men utilized for the quarterback and pitch.

5. There are four defenders aligned inside for the running game (again, an imaginary line is drawn through the outside shoulder of the offensive tackle). These defenders are responsible for the inside running attack of the option game.

6. There are four men stationed outside the tackles for the quarterback and pitch.

The Unbalanced Defense

The unbalanced defense (an example is indicated in *Diagram 3-3*) is any normal balanced defense that is either shifted over (forcing unit) or rotated (perimeter) to such an extreme as to create an unbalanced look. Most unbalanced defenses develop from the seven-man front schemes with the four deep secondary rotating before the snap of the football to a three deep and aligning a defender either on or near the line of scrimmage. The following are some of the alignment characteristics of the unbalanced defense.

1. It is usually an eight-man front—However, when an imaginary line is drawn through the center, 6 men are to one side of the center while 5 are on the other.

2. It is usually a three-deep defense—A four spoke rotates forward to create a three-deep secondary.

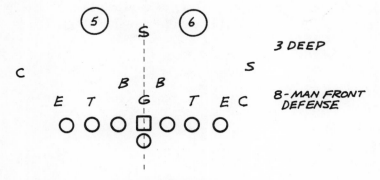

Diagram 3-3

The 5-4 defense is an example of a rotated four spoke secondary to a three deep. The cornerback is aligned on the line of scrimmage. There are 6 men right and 5 men aligned left. The offense should now gear its attack to the left.

3. It is an unbalanced defense—There are more defenders aligned on or near the line on one side than on the other.

TEACHING THE QUARTERBACK OPTION RESPONSIBILITIES OF DEFENSES

Once the quarterback has a general knowledge of defenses, he immediately is taught the techniques and responsibilities of the various defensive positions. With this overall understanding, he will recognize who (defender) is responsible for what (running back) on various options.

Defensive Responsibilities

Within the framework of each defense there are defenders assigned to the different phases of the option game *(Diagram 3-4)*. As previously stated, five defenders from the seven-man front defenses are responsible for the inside running game. Other defenders are designated for the quarterback and one of the rotated secondary defenders is established for the pitch. With the eight-man front defense, however, the four men inside are for the run. The four men aligned on or near the line outside are for both the quarterback and pitch. Other areas of responsibilities in all coverages are the flat and the deep one-third for the pass. In determining general characteristics and concepts of the various schemes necessary to halt the option game, the quarterback and coach can number the defensive personnel of all defenses. Through a quick count, therefore, the quarterback is knowledgable to the defenders responsible for the various levels of the option attack.

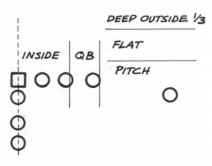

Diagram 3-4

The Numbering System

Defensive numbering is rather simple. The rules are as follows:

1. Count any man located directly over the center whether he is off or on the line of scrimmage as "0".
2. Count the remaining defenders from inside-out.
3. In any stack (or near stack) situation whether on or off the line of scrimmage, count the defender nearest the line for the lower of the two numbers.

Diagrams 3-5 through 3-8 illustrate four examples of defensive counting. Both seven-man and eight-man fronts are shown.

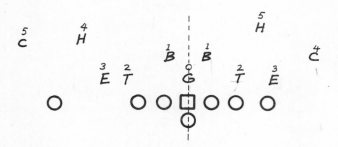

**An Odd 5-4 Defense
(Balanced Seven-Man Front)**

Diagram 3-5

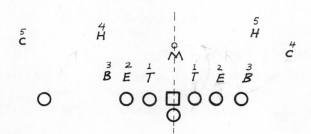

**An Even Pro-4 Defense
(Balanced Seven-Man Front)**

Diagram 3-6

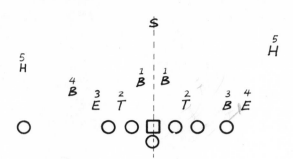

**An Even Split 4-4 Defense
(A Balanced Eight-Man Front)**

Diagram 3-7

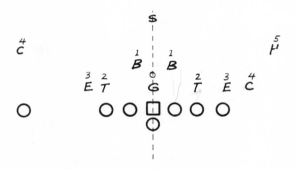

**An Odd 5-4 Defense
(An Unbalanced Eight-Man Front)**

Diagram 3-8

Responsibility of Defenders

Once the numbering system is known, the concept of which defenders are assigned to the various phases of the option game becomes quite clear. The following list indicates the fundamental responsibilities of each defense.

1. Numbers 1 and 2—Responsible for the Dive
2. Number 3—Responsible for the Quarterback
3. Number 4—Responsible for the Pitch or Trailing Halfback

4. Number 5—Responsible for any support of the pitch or quarterback. Number 5 also covers the deep outside one-third for the pass.

As the quarterback grasps these principles, he will recognize the defenders responsible for himself and the other backfield personnel. All that is required is to walk up behind the center and spot-check down the line where the play is directed. He can easily see defensive alignment, its characteristics, and the responsibility of each defender. He recognizes immediately that numbers one and two are responsible for any dive back into the line. He automatically adjusts to the defender responsible for himself. He can also detect the defender assigned to the pitch-back. He can now very intelligently attack any weaknesses that are relevant to the option game. He knows whom he must key on any inside or outside triple option. He can also easily spot the defensive man he is to option located on or off the line of scrimmage.

Stunt Changes

Once the quarterback understands defensive responsibility, he can easily see and understand the defensive changes that can occur after the ball is snapped. If the defense executes normally, then it is easier for the quarterback to read, key, and operate the option attack. However, once stunting materializes and responsibilities alter to strike the option attack, the quarterback must quickly react and properly read the actions of the defense.

The quarterback should comprehend the various stunts that can occur with various defenses. He should have a fundamental, but concise knowledge of stunts that can develop from the defenses he faces during a season. As games are planned during the week the quarterback should precisely understand the defenses he observes and the various stunts and blitzes that can prevent the option game from striking.

There are two levels of stunting that try to disrupt the option.

1. Forcing Unit Stunts
2. A Combination of Forcing Unit and Secondary Blitzes

Forcing Unit Stunts

Stunting can vary defensive responsibilities with the option. Two, three, or four-man stunts to one side of the line can easily result. The

Split 4-4 Defense is an example. *Diagram 3-9* illustrates the outside linebacker quickly stunting inside for any dive back or inside running game, even though the primary defense had him cover the quarterback.

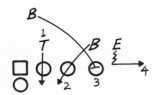

Stunt Changes Their Responsibility

Diagram 3-9

The inside linebacker is now free to move laterally along the line for the quarterback. The end still remains answerable to the pitch half-back. *Diagram 3-10* indicates another forcing unit assignment modification from the Split-4 Defense. The outside linebacker slants for the dive, but the defensive end now covers the quarterback. The inside linebacker shuffles quickly outside for the pitch, while the defensive halfback supports him. Another stunt is with the outside defenders *(Diagram 3-11)*. The defensive end forces inside for the quarterback as the outside linebacker and tackle are still accountable for the diving back. There are a number of other examples of various defenses and their stunts. The Split-4 serves as an example of how defenses change assignments to confuse the offense. As the quarterback and other personnel understand these deviations, the more proficiently the option attack will execute.

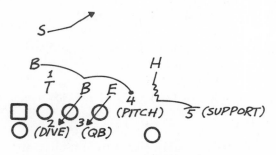

Diagram 3-10

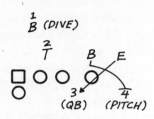

Diagram 3-11

Combination Stunts Between the Forcing Unit and Secondary

Various stunts can be used in hopes of confusing the offensive personnel at the perimeter level. Secondary stunts can easily occur from this area, with the defenders responsible for the quarterback and pitch. With these blitzes, other combinations can be added inside. In many cases, the quarterback, backs, and linemen read most of these stunts before the snap, since proper alignments play an important role for the defense. *Diagram 3-12* indicates a corner-fire between the defensive end, tackle, and safety from the 5-4 defense. The inside tackle and linebacker are responsible for the dive, while the safety covers the quarterback and the defensive end controls the pitch-back. With this overall knowledge of defenses and their option responsibilities, therefore, the quarterback can operate the option attack with intelligence and proficiency.

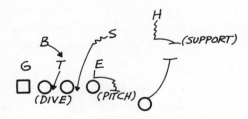

Diagram 3-12

KNOWLEDGE OF STRENGTHS AND WEAKNESSES OF DEFENSES

As the quarterback is taught the general structures and the option responsibilities of defenses, the coach works closely to teach him the strengths and weaknesses of defenses also. To train and clarify these concepts of strength, weaknesses, and how to attack defenses refer to the book *The Directory of Football Defenses* (West Nyack, N.Y.: Parker Publishing Company), written by the author. A thorough knowledge and understanding of defenses is essential for the quarterback. His ability to attack defenses strategically on the field can be the difference between success and failure. *Diagram 3-13 through 3-15* illustrate the three most often used defenses with strengths, weaknesses, and the areas to attack for each one.

THE 5-4 DEFENSE

Strengths: The 5-4 is an excellent running, pursuing, and containing defense. It is a nine-man front with quick rotational secondary coverage. The hook and flat areas are well covered. If the linebackers are strong, the defense is good. Various stunts can be used.

Weaknesses: Over the middle and guard area. The off-tackle can be weak with double team blocks. Various angle and option blocking can create weaknesses.

Attack: The offense should attack inferior personnel. The middle area can be attacked with straight, cross, and power blocking. Veering backs against pursuit is helpful. Double team blocking at the off-tackle hole is beneficial. Various option blocks can be used. Counters and scissors versus linebacker flow are helpful. Numerous option attacks go well versus the 5-4. This is due to the various blocking combinations in and outside. Triple options both at the end and corner areas can be accomplished. The swing and belly options are beneficial also.

THE PRO-4 DEFENSE

Strengths: The defense is strong over the guard, tackle, and end areas. It is a nine-man front with quick rotational coverage. It is excellent for the passing game (covering and rush).

Weaknesses: The defense is limited to one linebacker flowing. The middle area and at the off-tackle hole with various blocking combinations.

Attack: The offense can strike along the line with straight, cross, and trap blocking. Trapping can be accomplished on both the defense tackle and end. The defensive outside linebacker can

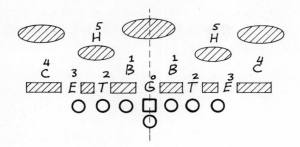

The 5-4 Defense

Diagram 3-13

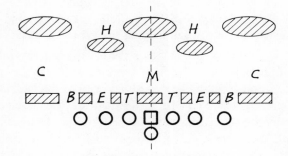

The Pro-4 Defense

Diagram 3-14

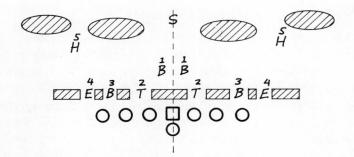

The Split 4-4 Defense

Diagram 3-15

be attacked with options with double teaming and other option blocking achieved on the defensive end and middle linebacker. Triple and regular options are excellent considerations.

THE SPLIT 4-4 DEFENSE

Strengths: Good linebacker personnel make the defense strong. It is strong over the center-guard area due to the four-on-three ratio. It is an excellent pursuing (linebackers) and containing defense. Excellent for stunting and penetration. Underneath pass coverage (four linebackers) and the three deep make it good against the pass.

Weaknesses: The middle area can be attacked quickly with certain blocking combinations. The area over the offensive tackle can be attacked. Formations can create weaknesses (twins). The flat is weak. If the secondary rotates, other pass weaknesses quickly develop. The middle, off-tackle, and inside the defensive end are weak against the power game.

Attack: The offense should attack the middle quickly with straight and trap blocking. Folding combinations can be used also. Sneaks and counters are good against the linebackers. Blocking combinations can be geared toward the defensive tackle and linebacker. If the defensive tackle can be reached by the guard, the offense has a distinct advantage. Various options can be used. The offense should use split ends and wide formations forcing the outside linebackers to align deeper for the pass. This greatly assists the option game, both triple and regular.

FORMATION, MOTION, AND SHIFTING

The quarterback should have a knowledge of formations, shifting, and motion variations, as well as their effect on a defense. Many alterations of these are effective in stopping stunts, such as the excellent example shown in *Diagram 3-16.* If the offense can't cope adequately with a corner stunt from a Split 4-4 Defense, the quarterback should send two receivers wide to one side. If the defender does not go out to cover these receivers in the flat, the ball should be thrown. However, if the defender does drop off the line, the quarterback has a better opportunity to execute the option game. Motion and shifting will also accomplish similar results.

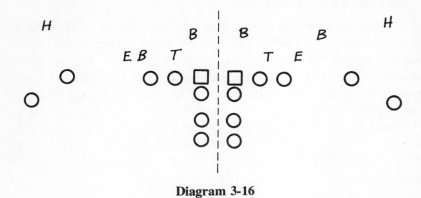

Diagram 3-16

KNOWLEDGE OF BACKFIELD MANEUVERS AND RESPONSIBILITIES

Most quarterbacks know the paths of the backs to whom he either fakes or hands-off. Knowledge of the backs' blocking assignments with the plays is also essential. With a few options, backs are responsible to block defenders assigned to the quarterback. In other instances they are needed to cut-off pursuit or block on the perimeter. Whatever the case may be, the quarterback should have a knowledge of the blocks being performed so he understands what to expect once he is in option territory.

KNOWLEDGE OF BLOCKING SCHEMES

It also becomes significant for the quarterback to have an idea of the blocking combinations that can result with the line. Offensive line rules are not necessarily important to know, but the overall blocking scheme should be understood. The quarterback should be aware of, for example, whether or not a double team is occuring at the off-tackle hole. If one does and he is optioning at that point, he has a better opportunity to keep the football. However, if a single block is employed, the opportunity to run has been slightly reduced.

Because of the blocking scheme, the halfback or fullback is, at times, asked to block a defensive lineman. If the quarterback is also going to fake, he may have to alter his running path slightly, if the defense has a stunt and a back must block at a different point along the line.

ATTACKING PERSONNEL

If the coach and quarterback can detect any personnel weaknesses of the defense, the option will operate better. For example, if the linebackers are not as strong inside, the quarterback may desire the inside running game. If the defensive end is slow, the quarterback may wish to attack the end's weaknesses often. If the defense is strong up the middle and off-tackle, the quarterback may have to attack the defensive perimeter with options. Whatever the case may be, the quarterback and coach should view films in advance and attempt to determine what personnel should be attacked first. Observations during the game may verify or alter these decisions also.

MENTAL PREPARATIONS AND TRAINING

It is essential that every aspect of the option game be clearly taught and drilled before anything is operated on the field. This requires many hours of preparation for the coach before he even deals with his quarterbacks. Once the groundwork and organization has been accomplished, he must teach and relate it to the quarterback properly.

Check Lists

It is a good idea for the coach to provide a checklist of everything taught to the quarterback. A partial sample of a checklist is illustrated in *Diagram 3-17*.

Monthly Time Schedules

It is important the coach have a monthly time schedule so what is to be accomplished is done in the time allotted. These schedules can be set for the season as well as the off-season periods. For example, the month of January may indicate blackboard meetings on defensive structure. February may show strengths and weaknesses of defenses and training films on the swing option. This can be continued every month. Anything appropriate for a particular span can be examined with the checklist.

Weekly and Daily Schedules

Weekly and daily schedules can now be designed and organized for the teaching and drilling of the quarterback. Setting time schedules (an hour a day, three days a week in the off-season) is an example. Of course, meetings during the season includes additional and pertinent information.

QUARTERBACK OPTION CHECKLIST

1. Defensive Structure
    a. Alignment characteristics of:
        1) The Seven-Man Front
        2) The Eight-Man Front
        3) The Unbalanced Front
    b. Numbering System
        1) Numbering system and option responsibilities of defenders
    c. Stunt Changes
        1) The Forcing Unit
        2) In Combination with the Secondary
            a) The 5-4 Defense
            b) The Pro-4 Defense
            c) The Split-4 Defense
            d) The Wide Tackle-6 Defense
            e) Combination of the Split-4 and Wide-6
            f) The 5-3 Wide
            g) The 5-3 Tight
            h) The 6-5 Goal

Diagram 3-17

BLACKBOARD DRILLS

Using the blackboard or overhead projector is a necessary item for the coach. He should explain everything encompassing the option game to the quarterback. Transparent overlays are beneficial and valuable time is not wasted. Employing slides when appropriate may be helpful.

During the drilling period it is profitable to have the quarterback stand in front of the group and explain in detail the various aspects of defenses and the option attack. This serves as a continuous reinforcement pattern for learning option strategy.

TRAINING FILMS

Training films are a major teaching aid for the option game. The quarterback can actually view what has been taught. He can readily witness the blocking schemes, the individual play of the defensive personnel, the various stunts, the courses of defensive ends, and the footwork and ball handling of the quarterback in relationship to the offensive backs. The training films are beneficial also because the quarterback can observe the same defense and option over and over again. He views the detailed coaching points that can occur which may not be mentioned previously in the meetings.

GAME FILMS

Viewing game films can be excellent also. Not only are the individual plays indicated, but the defenses and field strategy are also shown. All the game films during the past year or more can be viewed.

FIELD STRATEGY

Field strategy and ball position can be very important. It is the philosophy of the coach that must be instilled into the quarterback. Some coaches believe you can run the option anywhere on the field. The Wishbone and Split Veer offenses prove this. However, if a team does not execute the option that often, it may choose not to run the option with the coming-out offense or when going in for the score. Whatever the case may be, the coach should make it clear to the quarterback what he wants accomplished with the option aspect and field position. Down and distance are essential also. Does the coach want to run an option play with third or fourth and short yardage? Or would he rather run power in that situation? Another aspect to the option is wasting or conserving time. Does the coach want the option called with little time remaining in a game with the team in the lead? The same holds true when behind with little time remaining. The coach must make a great number of decisions and all of these must be prepared beforehand so the quarterback can make intelligent and sound decisions when the opportunity presents itself.

4

OPTION BLOCKING
SCHEMES

Precise blocking is essential for the success of any option. Without adequate blocking from the offensive line, yardage will be curtailed. In many instances the speed and quickness of the offensive backs will promote the blocks along the line. However, the less speed, quickness, and ability the backs possess, the more important the various blocking schemes become.

There are a number of blocking combinations utilized with the option attack. This chapter deals strictly with the leading blocks for most option plays. Other plays within a series, such as the straight dive or counter action inside, are not explained. Moderately used blocking schemes, rules, and coaching points, plus other aspects of non-option plays are mentioned within each of their respective chapters.

PRINCIPLES OF BLOCKING RULES

There are numerous rules and rule definitions favored by all coaches. The blocking rules that follow are rather easy to learn and fit any offensive attack with simplicity. Some principles and definitions must be digested first so the reader will have a complete knowledge of the rule presented. The rules are either by numbers or by a word description. The following must be perceived and understood:

1. Number defenders from inside-out.
2. If two defenders are stacked, the highest number of the two is the down lineman.
3. "Odd" call by center.
4. If a lineman is completely uncovered, no number is assigned for him (Example—Center and a Wide Tackle-6; Tackle with a Split 4-4).

The Numbering System

The offensive line counts the defenders from inside-out, i.e., from the center out to the end. *Diagram 4-1* illustrates the numbering system of the three primary defenses. Any man aligned over the center is #0. This is known as an "Odd" defense. This is essential to remember for reasons explained following. If a defender is not stationed directly over the center it is known as an even defense. The fundamental rules, therefore, are as follows:

1. Center   — Block #0
2. Guards   — Block #1
3. Tackles   — Block #2
4. Ends   — Block #3

As can be seen, if the entire line struck its assignment, a one-on-one block would occur. Of course this never is used, so certain linemen will be given word description rules to fit the block needed.

Changing Blocking Schemes by the "Odd" Call

This is a rather simple method to be utilized by the center and guard to alter blocking combinations slightly. The center barks the call on the line when he can reach the defender aligned either on or off the line of scrimmage. To illustrate, *Diagram 4-2* shows the blocking on the left with 1-2-3 blocking and on the right with an "Odd" call versus the Split 4-4 and Gap-Stack Defense.

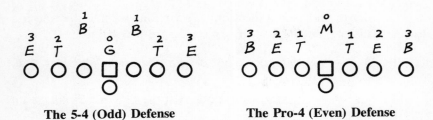

The 5-4 (Odd) Defense   The Pro-4 (Even) Defense

The Split 4-4 (Even) Defense

Diagram 4-1

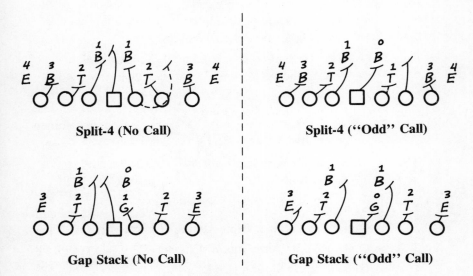

Split-4 (No Call)   Split-4 ("Odd" Call)

Gap Stack (No Call)   Gap Stack ("Odd" Call)

Diagram 4-2

Definition of Terminology

In order to understand the word descriptions set into the rule for the remainder of the chapter, the following are the definitions.

1. Over—Any defender aligned from the inside shoulder to a head-up alignment.
2. LB—Any linebacker positioned off the line of scrimmage in the immediate vicinity.
3. Inside—Any defender stationed on the line inside up to the head of the next offensive blocker.
4. PSG—Playside Gap—A technique and rule for the lineman to step to the gap on the playside before blocking rule.
5. Release—Release from the line and block rule indicated.
6. Out—A defender aligned from the outside shoulder to the inside shoulder of the next blocker positioned outside.

BLOCKING RULES

While any rule can be designated in any manner the rules will be indicated with letters.

Rule A — One-on-one blocking and double team techniques at the off-tackle position. This will be determined according to the defensive alignment.

Rule B — Strictly one-on-one blocking with a blocker releasing to the perimeter. A fake is usually realized inside.

Rule C — Triple Option Blocking

BLOCKING RULE A

Blocking rule A is illustrated in *Diagram 4-3*. The various options that use this rule are as follows:

1. The Swing Option (Chapter 8)
2. The Outside Wishbone Triple Option (Chapter 6)
3. The Outside Split-Veer Option (Chapter 7)
4. The Outside Belly Option (Chapter 9)
5. The Halfback Roll (Lead) Triple Option (Chapter 10)

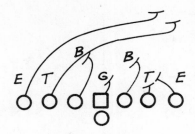

Blocking Rule A
(Versus the 5-4 Defense)

Diagram 4-3

IMPORTANT COACHING POINTS

Suitable splits with the blocking rule should be taken along the line of scrimmage. The block (double team) at the point of attack must be secured. The defender cannot penetrate across the line or force the double team to split. The backside of the line seal their defenders away from the hole. This is especially significant with the outside belly and wishbone option. If the ball is handed to the runner inside, he may react to pursuit and cut backside. Any crossfield blocking by offside lineman is beneficial also.

RULES (Diagram 4-4 Illustrates Various Defenses)

The line rules for the individual positions are as follows:

Frontside End—Over, LB, Inside
Frontside Tackle—#2
Frontside Guard—PSG, #1

Center—PSG, #0

Backside Guard—PSG, #1
Backside Tackle—PSG, Release for the Deep Outside 1/3
Backside End—Release for the Middle 1/3

TECHNIQUES

Frontside End—If a defender is aligned "over," the end strikes him through the numbers. If any stunt occurs, he remains in contact with

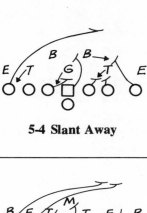

5-4 Slant Away

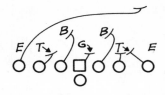

5-4 Slant Toward

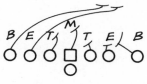

Pro-4

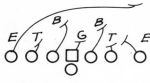

"Odd" Call Gap Stack

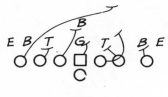

5-3

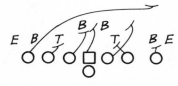

Possible "Odd" Call Split-4

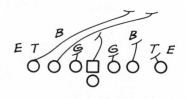

Wide-6 "Odd" Call

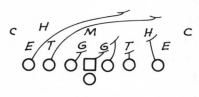

6-5 Goal Line

Blocking Rule A to the Right
Versus Various Defenses

Diagram 4-4

him. If a linebacker is in the area the end drives his face through the numbers and attempts to seal him inside. If the linebacker stunts forward, the end places his head in front so that penetration is halted. When there are no defenders either "over" or in an "LB" position, end lead-steps inside and doubles with the offensive tackle. He holds his head up and scans for stunts as he shoots for the double team. If a stunt doesn't materialize, he explodes his shoulders into the defender and drives him backward. If the defender scoops inside and disappears, the end reacts upfield for linebacker stunts.

Frontside Tackle—The tackle blocks number 2 wherever the man is aligned. If the defender is on the line, the tackle strikes a post block for the offensive end. He mustn't allow penetration in either direction. His body stabilizes in the middle. Once the tackle feels pressure from the offensive end, he slides his outside hip into the end's inside hip so the defender cannot split the double team block. When a defender is stationed directly over the tight end, the tackle singlely blocks his rule. If a linebacker is set over him (Wide-6), he attacks him by driving his face mask through the outside portion of the numbers. If it is a regular 4-3 defense, however, a double team is created with the tight end.

Frontside Guard—The guard is responsible for the gap to the playside first. He steps in that direction before blocking his assignment (number 1). As an example, the 5-4 slant defense can scoop the defensive tackle inside. If this develops (the playside gap), the guard blocks him with the offensive tackle. If the tackle does not arrive, however, he drives on for the linebacker. Versus the Split 4-4 Defense, it is dependent upon the call of the center. If a call is not sounded, he blocks the number 1 man by pulling around. If an "Odd" call is presented, though, he attempts to reach and sustain the defensive tackle. His main objective is to stop penetration before shooting for position.

Center—The center's first assignment is to lead-step toward the playside gap for any stunt. If a stunt does not transpire, he propels forward and blocks number 0 man. If a number 0 isn't present, he seals any other defenders away from the play. He should be prepared to block any slant or stunting linebackers. If the middle guard from a 5-4 Defense slants opposite the playside, the center automatically continues forward on his course and blocks the backside linebacker. Anytime he strikes a linebacker he should try to sustain him slightly higher.

Backside Guard—The guard's assignment is to lead to the playside gap first for any slant or stunt. If a middle guard scoops his way, he must shoot his head in front of him. If a linebacker stunts in the gap, from any defense, he should be prepared to halt him also. When stunts do not occur, he can block his number 1 man. He attacks him with a shoulder block and seals him away from the action.

Backside Tackle—At the outset, a lead-step is originated toward the playside gap for developing slants or stunts. If defenders do not appear, he releases across field and blocks the secondary defender responsible for the deep outside one-third of the field. His course should be as shallow as possible so he has the opportunity to set in front of the defender.

Backside End—He releases inside quickly and aims across the field also. As he nears the secondary defender, he aims his body in the direction the defensive halfback is moving and attempts to bowl him over.

OTHER BLOCKING COMBINATIONS

The Bump Technique

This technique is used by the offensive end and tackle versus various Seven-Man fronts where sealing linebackers is essential. When the linebacker cannot be blocked by the guard or center, the bump technique is applied. The bump is geared for the split-veer and wishbone triple options. The end splits approximately three feet from the tackle and at the snap of the ball steps inside at a 45 degree angle. If the defensive tackle loops out or reacts quickly in that direction, the end double teams with the tackle. However, if the offensive tackle alone can block the defender, the end then pivots upfield to seal the linebacker away from the hole *(Diagram 4-5)*.

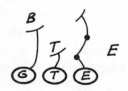

The Bump Technique

Diagram 4-5

The Swipe Technique

The swipe technique is similar to the bump. However, the end does not drive inside quite as much. This is exploited to a high degree with the swing option. In this case, the end releases almost directly upfield to seal linebacker flow. Only if the tackle loops so far outside does the end assist the tackle *(Diagram 4-6)*. If the defensive end crosses the end's face as he releases (a slant stunt), the end remains with him.

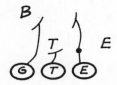

The Swipe Technique

Diagram 4-6

The Reach Technique

A reach tactic is employed for the swing option as well. It can only be executed versus a defense that has the guard uncovered (5-4, Gap-Stack, 6-5, etc.). In this situation, the offensive end releases from the line and never considers blocking any down lineman whatsoever. His main objective is the linebacker inside. The offensive guard and tackle must now execute a block against the defensive tackle. The blocking tackle launches an exaggerated lead-step outside on the snap. His main concern is halting any looping movement outside by the defender. The guard is taught to reach the outside leg of the defender.

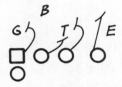

The Reach Block

Diagram 4-7

While this may be virtually impossible, it does force him to concentrate and release across the defensive tackle. His responsibility is to stop the slant and/or any penetration by the defender. Once both the guard and tackle reach outside, they attempt to use shoulder blocks and double team the defender *(Diagram 4-7)*. The great disadvantage of the reach is the opening that develops directly over the guard area. If the linebacker stunts forward, he could disrupt the play.

BLOCKING RULE B

Blocking rule B is illustrated in *Diagram 4-8*. It is mobilized for regular options directed at the defensive end. Options that utilize the B rule are:

1. The regular option from the Wishbone—not the Triple Option—(Chapter 6)
2. The counter option from the Wishbone (Chapter 6)
3. The regular option from the Split-Veer (Chapter 7)
4. The counter-option from the Split-Veer (Chapter 7)
5. The Split-T Option (Chapter 11)
6. The Isolation Option (Chapter 12)

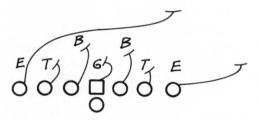

Blocking Rule B
(Versus the 5-4 Defense)

Diagram 4-8

IMPORTANT COACHING POINTS

The back faking through the middle area assists the offensive line blocking. Faking helps hold blocks slightly longer. The block of the frontside offensive tackle is essential. He must stop all penetration by this man. While the same rule applies for quick and/or counter plays, there is a difference in backfield timing. Because of this, the tackle's block varies in style and technique. On a quick faking dive and option at the end, the tackle's block is low and aggressive. Counter action requires slightly longer execution and, therefore, the block of the offensive tackle is more controlled.

The block of the end becomes significant when the ball is pitched. He has to remain off the ground and continue with his assignment. Penetration by other defenders along the line must be halted.

RULES (Diagram 4-9 Illustrates Defenses)

The individual rules for blocking rule B are as follows:

Frontside End—Release and Block Corner
Frontside Tackle—Over, Outside
Frontside Guard—PSG, #1

Center—PSG, #0

Backside Guard—PSG, #1
Backside Tackle—PSG, #2
Backside End—Release and Block Deep Outside 1/3

TECHNIQUES

Frontside End—There are two techniques the frontside end can execute when releasing to the corner area. On quick, straight along the line options, the end lead-steps outside "reading" the defender responsible for the flat area. This is either the cornerback rotating forward or the invert. The end should run parallel along the line before moving upfield. Blocking in this area is indicated later in the chapter. Once the end reads the defensive coverage, he approaches the defender as quickly as possible. Approximately four yards from him, the end decelerates and sets in a good football position. He does not block until the defender reacts to the ball carrier. The end never initiates a cross-body block unless absolutely necessary. He should stabilize the defender by blocking high through the numbers and shoulders and remaining with him.

The second technique employed by the end is the "jab" versus

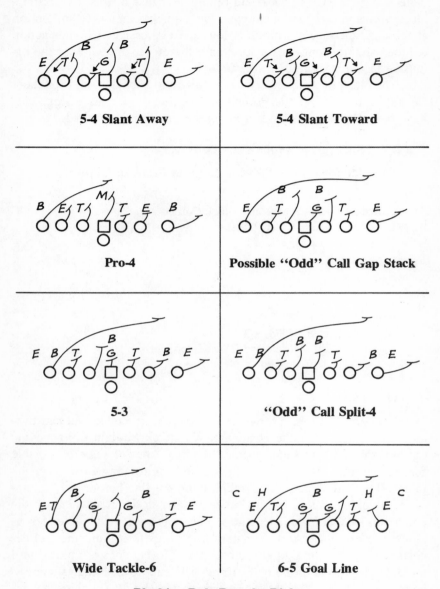

5-4 Slant Away

5-4 Slant Toward

Pro-4

Possible "Odd" Call Gap Stack

5-3

"Odd" Call Split-4

Wide Tackle-6

6-5 Goal Line

Blocking Rule B to the Right
Versus Various Defenses

Diagram 4-9

seven-man front defenses. This is used with any counter-action in the backfield. The end, on the snap of the ball, delivers a blow with the inside shoulder and forearm into the outside shoulder of the defensive end. As the job is executed, the end jerks the head up to read the secondary coverage. His shoulders remain parallel to the line and the feet are well underneath him. Once the end has jabbed the defender, he releases outside along the line as explained previously. The purpose of the jab is to slow any stunt that may occur by the defensive end because of the execution and faking of the counter plays in the backfield.

Frontside Tackle—When a defender is aligned "over," the tackle explodes from his stance and aims his shoulder through the outside numbers of the opponent's jersey. He must stabilize the defender. Position steps can cause major problems, especially when the defender explodes forward and penetrates. The inside fake freezes the defender on the line. If the defensive tackle scoops inside (an example is the 5-4 defense), the tackle continues forward and drives up through the linebacker. Once the defensive man is considered "outside," the tackle attacks him by lead-stepping in that direction. His head aims through the outside portion of the numbers and penetration cannot be permitted.

Frontside Guard—The guard steps toward the playside gap before blocking his rule, number 1. The step is dependent upon the defensive set. If a defender is "on," the guard aims his chest through the outside shoulder of the lineman but is prepared to block a linebacker, should the defender disappear inside. When a linebacker is positioned in the area, the guard aims toward the next lineman outside and is prepared to block any inside slant by this man. If a slant doesn't materialize, he continues for the linebacker and aims through the outside portion of the jersey numbers. The guard can use one of two techniques. He can remain with the linebacker to the conclusion of the play or he can jab the linebacker, then flatten his course along the line and block the defensive safety *(Diagram 4-10)*. He should be able to accomplish the jab because of the fake inside which freezes the linebacker.

Center—First the center lead steps to the playside gap scanning for any stunts. He blocks the number 0 man by aiming directly through his outside number. If the nose guard angles away from the option, he continues for the backside linebacker. Emphasis should be for the center to secure his block and not allow penetration. The fake of the

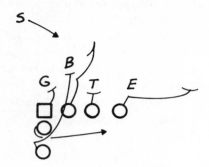

Diagram 4-10

back will assist him. The center should be aware of the counter-action used in the backfield, as reactions and movements of the defensive front alignment will vary because of this action. Since the play is designed outside, the center should make an "Odd" call versus an even defense whenever he has the opportunity.

Backside Guard—The playside gap is protected first by the guard. If a nose guard is aligned opposite the center, the guard blocks him if he slants in his direction. When his assignment (number 1) is aligned "over," he aims his shoulder through the inside portion of the numbers. A coaching point is implemented with the Split 4-4. As he approaches number 1 (linebacker), the guard can "swipe" the defensive tackle to assist the block of the backside tackle.

Backside Tackle—He is responsible for any slant or stunt to the playside gap. His next assignment is to block the number 2 defender. He should seal this defender and not permit him to pursue the play.

Backside End—The end releases across field for the defender responsible for the deep outside one-third of the field. He sprints a shallow course because of the forward reaction of the secondary to the option. He never glances at the option action and should throw a cross-body block once the defender reacts to the ball carrier.

OTHER BLOCKING COMBINATIONS

The Switch Block

The switch block is an excellent blocking scheme that can be utilized with any option play versus every defense. The purpose of the switch is to seal pursuit inside so the quarterback and trail halfback have a better opportunity to swing upfield to the corner. The end and tackle just switch assignments. This adjustment can be accomplished in the huddle or on the line. The end blocks the tackle's assignment and the tackle releases along the line to the corner. The block of the end is essential, because penetration by the defender cannot be tolerated. The farther away the end's assignment aligns, the more difficult it is to execute the block. *Diagram 4-11* illustrates the switch block versus seven-and-eight-man defensive fronts.

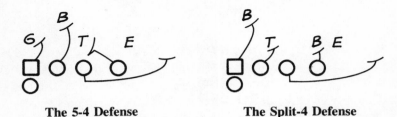

The 5-4 Defense   The Split-4 Defense

The Switch Block

Diagram 4-11

The Pull Technique

The pull blocking scheme is useful against any situation where the guard can pull out of the line (5-4, Gap Stack, 6-5, etc.). This is practiced with any quick, along-the-line option, such as the split-veer or wishbone. The purpose of the blocking scheme *(Diagram 4-12)* is to seal linebackers inside and still establish a blocker in the flat area. As indicated, the end uses a seal technique against the linebacker, while the offensive tackle aims through the outside shoulder of the defensive tackle. If the defender scoops inside, the responsibility to block him

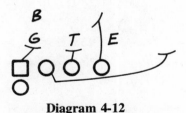

Diagram 4-12

lies with the diving back. The tackle then continues for the linebacker. The guard pulls, escapes the defensive end, and blocks the corner or flat area. Everyone else remains with his rules and techniques.

Double Team Blocking

Double team blocking can be realized in the middle area in any situation when a defender is aligned in one of the gaps. The center and guard, but more often the guard and tackle, can double team. *Diagram 4-13* illustrates the double team block. The faking ball carrier is now responsible for the linebacker.

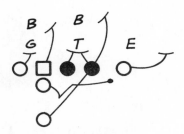

Diagram 4-13

Isolation Block

An excellent blocking scheme for the isolation option (described in Chapter 12) is shown against the 5-4 defense in *Diagram 4-14*. Since the inside isolation play is blocked in this manner, the double team block geared at the center can freeze the linebacker and force him to set forward, where the fullback blocks him. All the other blocking assignments and techniques of rule B remain the same.

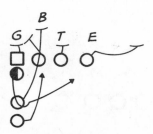

Diagram 4-14

The Horn Technique

The ''Horn'' technique is utilized on any counter action with the blocking rule. It is helpful when blocking linebackers. The technique can be a fundamental block within the rule or can be declared on the line of scrimmage. It can be used against various defenses i.e., 4-4, 5-4, 5-3, etc. The end releases normally. The offensive tackle blocks his defender wherever he flows. The guard jabs out along the line and keys his assigned linebacker for stunt. If the linebacker shoots forward, the guard rams through the defender's numbers and doesn't allow penetration. If the linebacker reacts quickly outside, the guard attacks him according to the movement of the defensive tackle. If the tackle slants inside (5-4 or 5-3 Defense) the guard pulls around, but if the tackle loops outside, the guard drives upfield for the linebacker as previously executed *(Diagram 4-15)*.

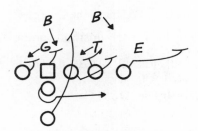

The Horn Technique Versus the 5-3 Defense

Diagram 4-15

BLOCKING RULE C

Blocking rule C is shown in *Diagram 4-16*. The options that profit from this rule are the following:

1. The Wishbone Triple Option (Chapter 6)
2. The Split-Veer Triple Option (Chapter 7)

IMPORTANT COACHING POINTS

Proper splitting is essential for successful blocking. The line should start with maximum splits where possible. Usually this is a 2½-3 foot split for the guard, 3 foot for the tackle and 3-3½ foot split for the end. The splits can easily adjust when the situation arises.

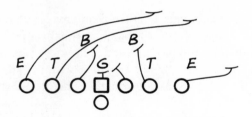

Blocking Rule C

(Versus the 5-4 Defense)

Diagram 4-16

Movement and sealing defenders at the point of attack are essential. The block by the releasing end is important once the pitch is executed.

RULES (Diagram 4-17 Illustrates the Defenses)

The individual rules for the positions are as follows:

Frontside End—LB, Release and Block Corner
Frontside Tackle—LB Inside
Frontside Guard—Inside, Over, Out

Center—#0 (Post) (Automatic Odd Call)

Backside Guard—PSG, #1
Backside Tackle—PSG, Release for Deep Outside 1/3
Backside End—Release for Deep Middle 1/3

TECHNIQUES

Frontside End—The end releases in the same manner described for blocking rule B. He does not utilize a jab technique although a few teams do apply it. The end escapes the number three defender outside and immediately reads the secondary coverage.

Frontside Tackle—The tackle blocks the first linebacker aligned inside. His release from the line is dependent upon the defense. If a defensive lineman is located directly over or slightly outside, the tackle scoops inside. If the defender sets inside, the tackle releases outside of

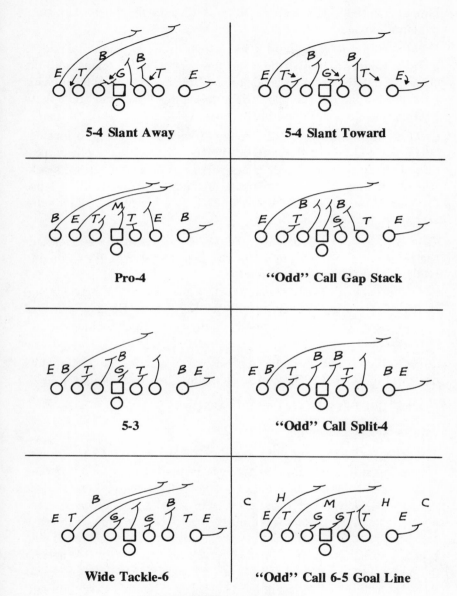

5-4 Slant Away

5-4 Slant Toward

Pro-4

"Odd" Call Gap Stack

5-3

"Odd" Call Split-4

Wide Tackle-6

"Odd" Call 6-5 Goal Line

Blocking Rule C to the Right

Versus Various Defenses

Diagram 4-17

him and upfield. His responsibility is to stop the linebacker from pursuing outside.

Frontside Guard—The guard's first responsibility is inside. If a middle guard is aligned opposite the center the guard double teams with the center. If a defensive man is positioned ''over'' or ''out,'' he aims his face through the outside knee. He sustains this block and attempts to gain an outside position on him.

Center—The center blocks the number 0 man wherever he is located. When the middle guard is aligned directly ''over,'' he applies a post technique, since the frontside guard will assist on a double team block. It is noteworthy that the center bark an ''odd'' call when the defense merits it. If there is no ''0'' defender (Wide Tackle-6), the center helps secure the backside pursuit.

Backside Guard—The playside gap (scanning for slants or stunts) is the guard's number one priority. He then locates the number 1 defender and diverts him from the play.

Backside Tackle—The backside tackle lead-steps to the playside gap before releasing to the deep outside one-third of the field. It is critical that he release in front of the number 2 defender which includes a Split 4-4 tackle.

Backside End—The away end releases inside also for the deep middle one-third of the field. His course is shallow before swinging upfield.

OTHER BLOCKING COMBINATIONS

Outside Release Technique

This tactic is popular versus the 5-4 Defense, but can be used versus any seven-man front alignment. Instead of the tackle scooping inside for a linebacker, he releases outside. The purpose of this scheme is two fold. First it is an excellent way to achieve an out-side-in block on the inside linebacker for the quarterback keep or pitch. Second, it can be a beneficial defensive response for a hand-off to the diving back, especially when the defensive tackle reacts outside. Whatever the purpose of the play (hand-off or option), the offensive tackle has the responsibility of blocking the linebacker. The only exception is if the defensive tackle loops outside. If this occurs the blocker will remain with the tackle. The frontside guard now blocks the linebacker (in case of stunt), while the center leads to the playside gap *(Diagram 4-18)*.

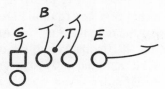

Diagram 4-18

CAT Block

The "C" and "T" of CAT indicate the blocking combination between the center and tackle. The purpose of this block (against the 5-4 Defense) is to either seal the middle guard with the center or assist with the backside linebacker. With the CAT block, the frontside guard can acquire a better angle to block the inside linebacker, also *(Diagram 4-19)*. The tackle aims behind the guard's lead-step so a collision does not result.

Diagram 4-19

Bump Technique

The outside bump technique was described with the "A" blocking rule. The same idea is utilized, however, but with the frontside guard and tackle. The bump is delegated to the tackle so the guard will have a better opportunity to block. The bump is adopted anytime a defensive lineman is aligned in the guard-tackle seam *(Diagram 4-20)*.

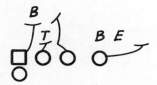

Diagram 4-20

The guard reaches the defender trying to arrive at an outside position on him. The tackle aims his first step (gaining ground) approximately a foot in front of the hip of the defensive tackle. At this point, the tackle pivots directly upfield for the linebacker. If the defensive tackle reacts quickly outside, the tackle automatically slams into him and doubles with the guard. If the defender doesn't react out quite as far, the blocker simply bumps him on the way to the linebacker. If, as he drives upfield he does not touch the defensive lineman, then it is immediately assumed the guard reached his assignment.

GET Block

The "G" and "T" of GET describes the blocking combination between the guard and tackle. The purpose of the double team is to secure the defensive tackle away from the option. This can be used against the Pro-4, Wide Tackle-6, 4-3, etc. *Diagram 4-21* illustrates the double team block versus the Pro-4 Defense.

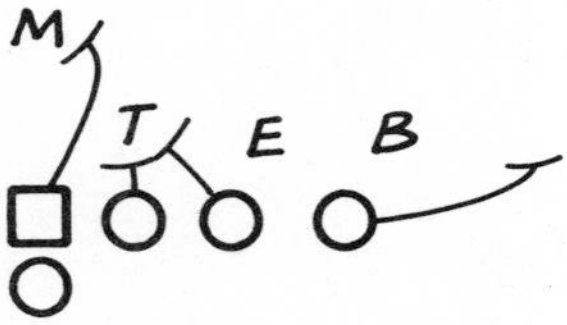

Diagram 4-21

5

PERIMETER BLOCKING FOR THE OPTION ATTACK

Option blocking at the perimeters of formations is essential. The blocking within this area is the point of attack for the pitch man, as well as the quarterback. If the quarterback keeps, most of his action is upfield and outside, removed from pursuit. Once the ball is tossed, the halfback must rely on perimeter blocking for ample running area.

BLOCKING AREA (ZONE BLOCKING)

There are two methods of blocking the perimeter, i.e., zone, or man-to-man. *Diagram 5-1* illustrates the corner areas the defense must defend, for both the pass and the option game. One defensive secondary man is responsible for the deep outside one-third of the field. Similar needs are required for the flat areas. Since defenders are most likely located in these areas, offensive personnel (wide-outs, ends, fullbacks, halfbacks, etc.) have to be assigned to block them. This is zone blocking. One offensive man blocks the deep outside one-third with another responsible for the flat.

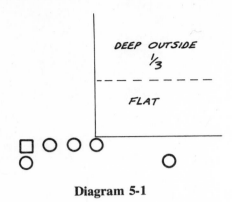

Diagram 5-1

Zone blocking is usually the better and more advantageous method of blocking, because the widest potential receiver continually drives upfield ten to fifteen yards. The defense will never know at the outset whether it is a pass or an option play. The following man-to-man method cannot attack in the same fashion because of certain secondary coverages (rotation, five underneath zone, etc.)

THE NUMBERING SYSTEM (MAN-TO-MAN BLOCKING)

An alternate method is man-to-man blocking. In order for the perimeter blockers to know their assignments faultlessly, a numbering system should be set up. The numbering is similar to that which the quarterback uses for reading purposes of option games. For the training of the quarterback, Chapter 3 indicated a count-off system from inside-out. Chapter 4 also described an inside-out approach for the blocking rules of linemen. The perimeter blocking rules, however, are exactly the opposite. Their numbering is outside-in. This is rather obvious. It is simpler for a wide-out receiver to count in this manner than to scan inside and attempt to count the defenders out. *Diagram 5-2* illustrates the assignment numbering for man-to-man blocking from various offensive formations. The wide-out is number 1 and the second blocker inside is responsible for number 2. While this is the easiest method of blocking, it is not always the best. If the wide receiver blocks number "1" but the defender rotates forward, the wide-out must halt his progression and block him. Eventually the defensive secondary can read the wide-out easily to determine a run or pass.

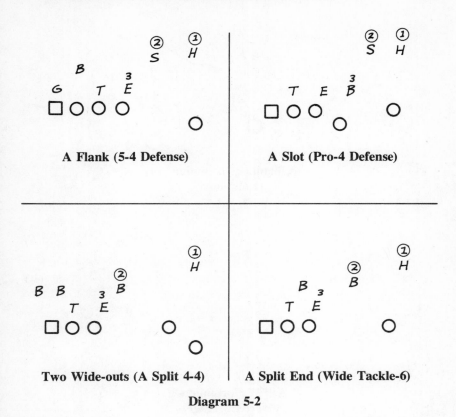

A Flank (5-4 Defense)

A Slot (Pro-4 Defense)

Two Wide-outs (A Split 4-4)

A Split End (Wide Tackle-6)

Diagram 5-2

ZONE BLOCKING OF THE DEEP OUTSIDE ONE-THIRD

An offensive receiver must be assigned to block the deep outside one-third of the field no matter what the coverage or the option. This blocker is always the *widest* man from the offensive set. It could be a flanker from a flank formation, an end split, or some variation of a slot, twins, etc. If a tight formation is called, i.e., the "T" or wishbone, the offensive end automatically becomes the widest receiver. In all cases, therefore, the widest man aligned in the offensive set is responsible for the deep outside one-third of the field with all option plays. *Diagram 5-3* illustrates three examples of a flanker, split end, and tight formation.

ZONE BLOCKING PRINCIPLES AT THE FLAT

There are certain precepts necessary when sending blockers to the flat area. These are:

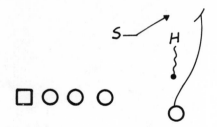

**A Flanker Formation
(Rotation)**

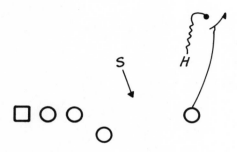

**A "T" Formation
(Invert Coverage)**

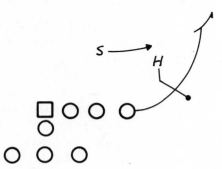

**A Slot Formation
(Rotation)**

Diagram 5-3

1. If no fake is initiated inside the offensive tackle, then all blocking at the perimeter is accomplished with the backfield personnel, i.e., flankers, halfbacks, fullbacks.

2. When any fake is established into the line, an offensive lineman or a third back must be sent to block at the perimeter (to substitute for the diving back). A blocker is not needed when the flat area is being optioned.

No Fakes Inside

Diagram 5-4 illustrates an example of no fake occurring. The line, therefore, seals the defensive front inside and away from the option with a back sent toward the flat (the swing option is an example).

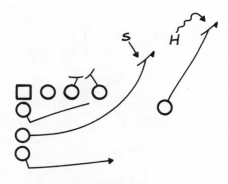

Diagram 5-4

A Fake Inside

Diagram 5-5 indicates various fakes inside. One of the lineman or the third back is now assigned to block the flat.

READING THE COVERAGE

Reading the defensive coverage is essential when blocking at the perimeter. Whoever is assigned to block the deep outside one-third and the flat areas should be well drilled. In some instances, blocking the defensive movement is simple. The defense sets in coverage and the blockers read it before the ball is ever snapped. However, if a defense is multiple and causes various secondary stunts, the blockers must read the coverage after the snap and while on the move.

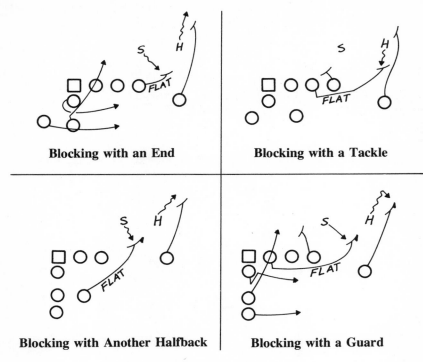

Blocking with an End

Blocking with a Tackle

Blocking with Another Halfback

Blocking with a Guard

Diagram 5-5

Reading by the Widest Receiver

The widest receiver aligns in his position and immediately attempts to interpret the coverage used. If he cannot discern it, he sprints quickly from the line at the snap of the ball. The first three steps should indicate his assignment. He merely reads the defender aligned over him. If the defender immediately scampers backward, the wide-out blocks him. If, however, the defender attempts to shove him, or begins to slow, the wide-out continues upfield and quickly scans inside. From experience he automatically knows a defender is sent from that direction to cover him. *Diagram 5-6* illustrates the read.

Reading by the Inside Blocker

The inside blocker (fullback, halfback, end, tackle, etc.) keys the next inside defender. When this defender stays or drives forward in any

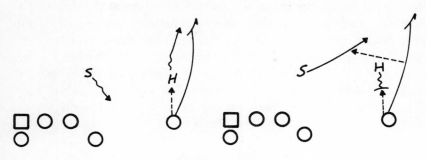

Diagram 5-6

The first read is indicated at the defensive half-back. He next scans inside for the safety.

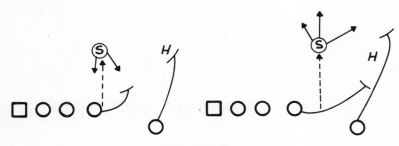

Diagram 5-7

manner, the inside blocker is responsible for him. If, however, the second defender inside (safety) goes backward or deep outside, the releasing blocker quickly shifts outside for the corner or other halfback *(Diagram 5-7)*.

BLOCKING TECHNIQUES BY THE WIDE-OUT (THE STALK BLOCK)

The techniques for the wide receiver, whether a flanker or split end, remain similar. At the snap of the ball, the wide-out releases on an outside course and drives downfield with as much speed as possible. With this burst from the line, the defender should view it as if it is a pass. The receiver continues as far as the defender back pedals. Once the defender begins to react forward, the wide-out immediately sets into a good football position and focuses his eyes on the defender's numbers. At this point the wide-out should have an outside position on the defender. *(Diagram 5-8)*. As the defender reacts forward, the wide-out strikes a blow into the numbers with a shoulder block. The arms and shoulders rise up to form a good blocking base. The feet are spread and well underneath the blocker. The knees are slightly bent with the hips low. The block should be as high as possible in an attempt to obstruct the view from the option.

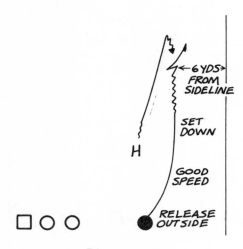

Diagram 5-8

Once the defender begins to slide away, the wide-out can throw a crossbody block at his knees. The block should not be made quickly. If the block is initiated too soon and the trailing back is late, the defender can easily gather himself, slide away from the block and make the tackle. At times it is better if the blocker decelerates early so he can block the defender also. When the wide-out explodes downfield, he should go no closer to the sideline than six yards. The back needs ample area to run outside and may have to cut inside if no room is sufficient to maneuver.

BLOCKING TECHNIQUES AT THE CORNER

The blocking techniques in the flat area depend to a great extent on where the blocker began. As mentioned previously, it could be an end, tackle, guard, fullback, or halfback. It also could be initiated from a wide-out position (twins formation).

Blocking Inside-Out (Arc Block)

Blocking from an inside-out approach is basically the same for the backs and lineman. The blocker releases from the line and escapes the defender to be optioned (defensive end). As he releases, he reads the coverage and the man he is responsible to block. Initially, he drives for width before depth. The reason is obvious. If he maneuvers for depth first *(Diagram 5-9)* he may have a poor angle on the defender. He cannot achieve an outside-in approach or block. By gaining width he has a better opportunity to get the outside-in position he wishes. As the releasing blocker maneuvers for width, he scans for the defender he is assigned on approximately the third step. He may be able to read the coverage before the snap of the ball. Whatever occurs, he approaches the defender and attempts to gain an outside position on him. He must sprint at full speed to achieve this relationship. Once he is within three to four yards of the defender, he sets into a good football position and blocks according to the defender's reactions. The block should be high and through the outside numbers. The shoulders and arms rise for good blocking stability, and the feet are well underneath him for a good blocking base *(Diagram 5-10)*. If the defender reacts quickly to the option before the arc blocker can set in a football position, he should continue upfield to obtain an outside-in position and, again, block high if possible. If, at any time, he loses his block, or the defender slides away, the blocker should aim at his knees to bowl him over.

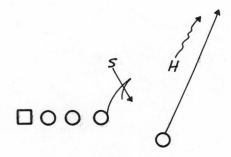

Diagram 5-9

He should achieve width before depth

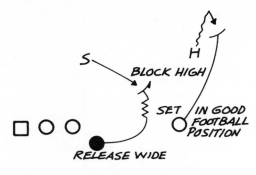

Diagram 5-10

When a back releases from the backfield, however, his relationship with the trailing back is entirely different. The trailing back is almost directly behind him. The blocking back does not have the time nor the opportunity to acquire a good football position. He lead-steps in the direction of the option and attempts to attain an outside position on the defender. He can read the coverage either before or after the snap of the ball. He arcs outside and aims for the outside hip of his assignment. The back continues on this path until he is close enough so he can aim both his shoulders and arms through the outside hip of the defender. He must topple him by rolling his inside shoulder into his hip and thigh and continue rolling until the assignment is completed *(Diagram 5-11)*.

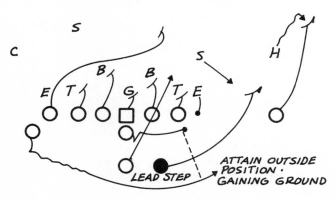

Diagram 5-11

There are times when the defender may scoot far outside in an attempt to contain the pitch halfback. Any arc block, therefore, to maintain an outside-in position cannot materialize. If this persists, the coaching point is quite simple. The blocker aims for an outside position until he views ''color'' flash past his face to his outside shoulder. (''Color'' is the jersey of his opponent.) As can be imagined, there is absolutely no technique the arc blocker can use to knock him inside. The lead blocker, now, performs a reverse crossbody block into the opposite hip of the defender and forces him outside. In many cases, this usually happens close to the sideline and the trail back must cut inside anyway at this juncture. The defender responsible for the pitch should be eliminated *(Diagram 5-12)*.

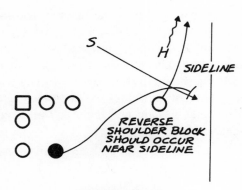

Diagram 5-12

The halfback attempts to achieve an outside-in block. Since the defensive safety flies so far wide, the halfback executes a reverse crossbody block.

BLOCKING OUTSIDE-IN (THE CRACK-BACK BLOCK)

The crack-back block is utilized by offensive blockers who are set wide, but are not the widest receivers in the formation. (Alternate blocking patterns are indicated at the end of the chapter.) The crack-back is slow in developing. The block is usually deployed against the walk-away defensive position. The defender can either be aligned or moving into the area *(Diagram 5-13)*. Before the snap, the blocker

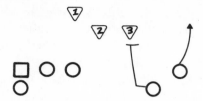

Diagram 5-13

should recognize the coverage. Once the play begins he pivots inside, progresses a couple of steps, and hesitates long enough to determine the target and his course. As the defender moves forward the blocker sets into position, sinks his hips, and prepares to block him. As the target sweeps within striking range, the blocker uncoils and explodes through the jersey numbers. It is essential that he not lunge at his target or strike below the belt line. Also, he must "stalk" the defender and not overly commit to him. The tempo of the block is determined by the play of the defender as shown in *Diagram 5-14*. The width of the split will control the course of the crack blocker also *(Diagram 5-14)*. *Diagram 5-15* illustrates the arc and the crack-back versus the three and four deep secondaries.

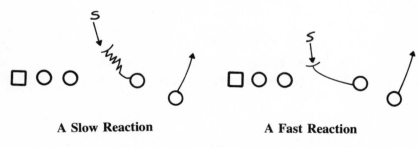

A Slow Reaction   **A Fast Reaction**

Diagram 5-14

BLOCKING THE DEFENDER IN A STUNTING POSITION

When a defender is located near the option area (defensive end), he is in a stunting position. Both the offensive line and the back must be prepared if a stunt occurs. A stunt can be anticipated and read before the ball is snapped. Once the ball is put into play the inside blocker

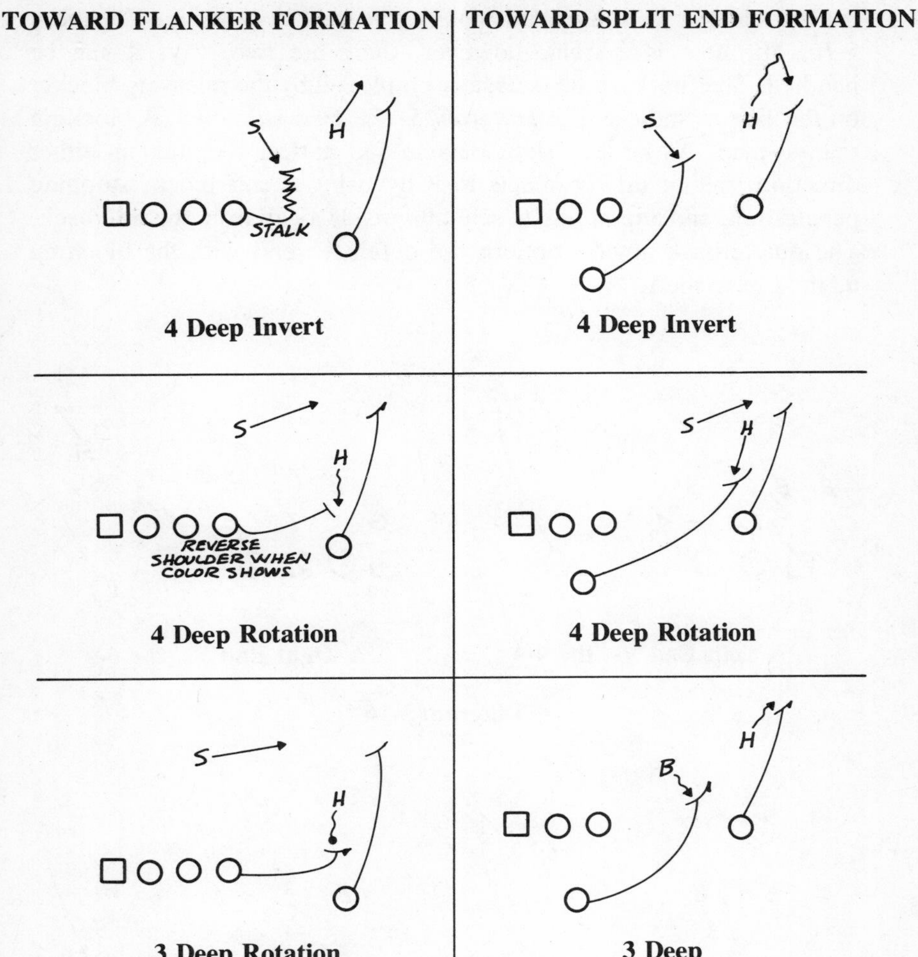
TOWARD FLANKER FORMATION
TOWARD SPLIT END FORMATION
S
H
STALK
4 Deep Invert
S
H
4 Deep Invert
S
H
REVERSE SHOULDER WHEN COLOR SHOWS
4 Deep Rotation
S
H
4 Deep Rotation
S
H
3 Deep Rotation
H
B
3 Deep
CRACK-BACK VERSUS 4 DEEP
CRACK-BACK VERSUS 3 DEEP
S
H
S
B
H

Diagram 5-15

releases and reads the possible stunt. If the stunt doesn't materialize, the arc blocker is in excellent position to seal him inside. *(Diagram 5-16)*. If there is a stunt, however, there are two ways it can be handled. The first method is usually employed by the releasing blocker on the line as indicated in *Diagram 5-17*. This is known as blocking man-to-man. As he lead-steps outside and notices the stunt in either direction (out or in), he reacts to it by using a butt block, stopping penetration, and attempting to seal him inside away from the trail back. The quarterback always options the defensive end with the blocking method described.

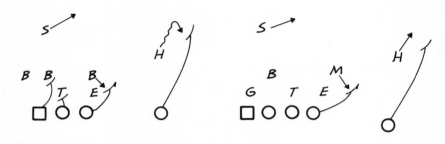

A Split End Vs. the 4-4   A Tight End Vs. the 5-4

Diagram 5-16

A Split End Vs. the 4-4   A Tight End Vs. the 5-4

Diagram 5-17

Another alternative is zone blocking. Whoever the blocker is, i.e., fullback, halfback, end, tackle, etc. he attacks the widest man that arrives on the line of scrimmage no matter who is the defender. In this situation the quarterback options the first defender that arrives past the offensive tackle's block. The blocker still follows his pre-designed course. His aims outside toward his assignment by placing his shoulder through the outside hip. *Diagram 5-18* illustrates four different blockers with both linemen and backs involved.

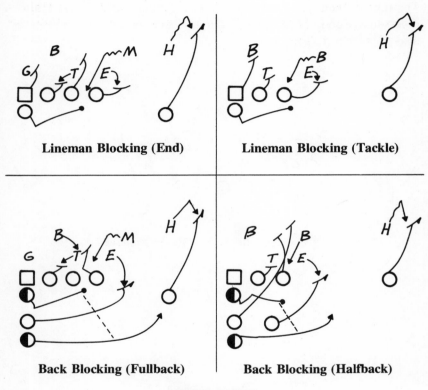

Lineman Blocking (End)	Lineman Blocking (Tackle)
Back Blocking (Fullback)	**Back Blocking (Halfback)**

Diagram 5-18

BLOCKING A DEFENDER ALIGNED DIRECTLY ON A WIDE-OUT

There are instances, directed toward either the flanker or split end, when a defender aligns opposite the wide-out receiver. Since the defender is wide by alignment, he is automatically in position to contain the pitch man. Unless he is on a stunt (usually not the case) or back pedals from the line, there is never an opportunity for the defender to be blocked inside. The wide-out releases from the line (forcing an outside release) and drives upfield as previously mentioned. The inside blocker lead-steps and aims outside toward the defender. As the blocker approaches, he should try to force an angle to knock the defender inside. However, if the defender resists and contains wide outside, the blocker merely blocks him high and shields him outside. The runner, then, can easily swerve inside before striking out again. A reverse crossbody block may be required to knock the defender away, also *(Diagram 5-19)*.

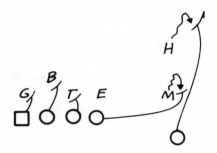

"Monster" Back Directly on Flanker

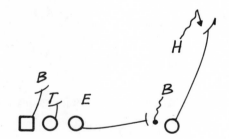

Linebacker Aligned Opposite Split End

Diagram 5-19

SWITCHING PERIMETER BLOCKS

The blocking described throughout this chapter has illustrated and explained a method of blocking the perimeter, i.e., the wide-out driving upfield with the inside blocker designated for the flat area. Another blocking scheme can be easily instituted. This can be done at any time. In some cases it may be better than the blocking employed. All that has to change are the assignments of the wide receiver and the next blocker set inside. Switching assignments can create blocking angles not previously presented. A simple word has only to be introduced to create this blocking pattern. Altering assignments can be achieved in the huddle or on the line. The wide-out now utilizes a crack-back technique, while the inside blocker widens and arcs his release. He aims for the outside hip of the widest defender (the man originally aligned opposite the wide-out). The blocker can either be the fullback, halfback, or any one of the down linemen. *Diagram 5-20 and 5-21* illustrate both a halfback and lineman executing this combination.

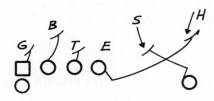

Diagram 5-20

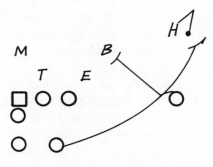

Diagram 5-21

If the wide-out's blocking assignment is well off the line, he can release downfield for two or three steps before turning inside toward his target. This forward movement assists the block of the inside man. The defender immediately will begin to back pedal and this added interval assists the inside blocker *(Diagram 5-22)*.

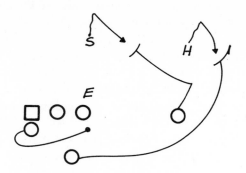

Diagram 5-22

Since the defensive safety is away from the line, the split end spurts upfield before sealing inside. A counter-action can be helpful also.

CALLING BLOCKING COMBINATIONS

Since there are various defensive secondary coverages for the passing and option game, using the proper perimeter blocking scheme at the point of attack can be very helpful. The coverage can sometimes be detected by the alignment of the secondary or the down and distance tendencies the defense maintains during a season. When the releasing blockers are wide and separated, the snap hand or foot signals can be added. If they are close (a twins' formation), a simple verbal call can be used.

There are many similarities to the various defensive coverages toward the side of the option. The coverages can either be zone (rotation or invert) or man-to-man. A rotational zone can be either regular rotation, five under two deep, or five under three deep. Whatever the alignment, however, it is still some form of rotation. With the various coverages, therefore, three different calls can be given to strategically block at the perimeter. The following are examples.

1. RUN—Regular blocking as described previously. The wide-out blocks the deep one-third while the inside blocker scans the flat.

2. SWITCH—Switching the assignments of both blockers.

3. FLY—If two receivers read man-to-man coverage, they both release and draw the defenders deep.

Diagram 5-23 through 5-25 illustrate and describe the various calls and blocks. The only call that could leave a defender free is the fly. (Man-to-man was viewed, but zone actually resulted.)

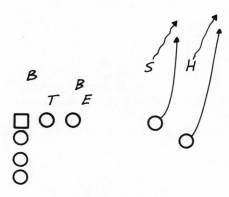

Diagram 5-23

A Fly is called. Man-to-man is read before the snap of the ball.

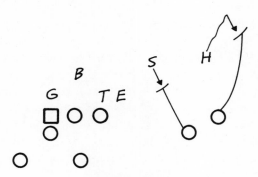

Diagram 5-24

A Run is called. An invert is indicated and the inside wide halfback is in excellent position to block him.

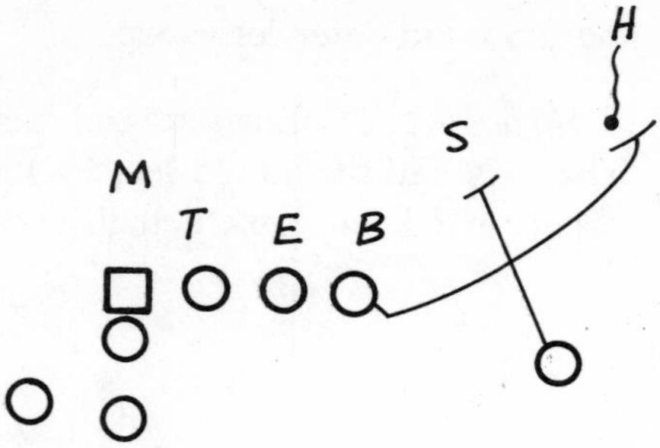

Diagram 5-25

A Switch is called. The safety threatens the outside pitch quickly and the defensive halfback is aligned deep.

6

THE WISHBONE TRIPLE OPTION

The wishbone triple-option series is one of football's most exciting offensive trends. It incorporates several simple but potent principles which place enormous pressure upon defenses. The triple option is geared to numerous formations, but the wishbone look and its national success has ranked it as one of the prominent sets today.

The objective of the wishbone triple option is to isolate the two defenders located outside the nose of the offensive tackle. It also forces them into various reactions and guessing games as to who will receive the football and where the ball will strike. The quarterback has the opportunity to present the ball to the diving fullback according to the reactions of the first defensive man. However, he can keep or pitch on the reactions of the next opponent (usually the defensive end). Since the purpose of the wishbone is to strike quickly, the defense has little time to react. The concept of releasing receivers from the line is also a valuable aid. It prevents the defense from knowing whether the play is a run or a pass. The secondary cannot react quickly toward the option to force the tackle. If there is reaction to the run, the quarterback can easily pass to one of his receivers.

With so many counters, counter options, etc., it is virtually impossible for the defense to pursue quickly. If it does, the counter game should be successful. If it holds position to cope with the threat of the pass and counter game, it creates additional defensive pressure on the offensive flow side.

WISHBONE ADVANTAGES

The advantages of the wishbone attack are as follows:

1. The only personnel that have to flip-flop from side to side are the split and tight ends. The interior line and backs remain the same.

2. The plays are easy to learn and there is enough time to practice for consistent and necessary repetitions.

3. It is a mirrored attack. The same play to the right can be executed left.

4. It is a goal line to goal line offense. The offensive formations and plays do not change because of field position.

5. The offense does not depend upon the passing game.

6. In order for the defense to cover the triple option adequately, the split end can only be covered one-on-one.

7. The play action pass becomes a valuable weapon for the offense.

8. The defense has only one practice week to prepare for the wishbone, while the wishbone has been practicing every day.

9. The game plan remains constant. This allows the offense to practice their techniques consistently and against various defenses.

10. It forces the defense to play responsibility. Defenders have to be responsible for the fullback, quarterback, and trailing halfback on either side of the center.

11. The wishbone attack can operate to either the tight end or split end.

FORMATIONS

Diagram 6-1 illustrates the basic formation. The fullback aligns directly behind the quarterback, while the two halfbacks set slightly deeper and behind their offensive guards. A split end is stationed to one side. The wishbone triple option always begins with the fullback driving through the guard-tackle gap. Other formations can be used with the same principle, also. As long as a fullback is set behind the quarterback and a halfback is in position for the pitch, any formation can be used. *Diagram 6-2 through 6-4* illustrate various formations other than the traditional wishbone.

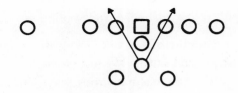

Diagram 6-1

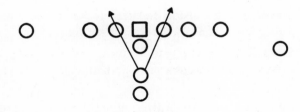

I Formation

Diagram 6-2

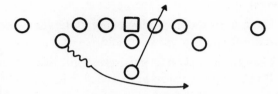

Automatic Motion

Diagram 6-3

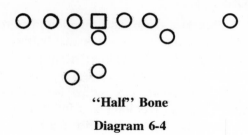

"Half" Bone

Diagram 6-4

STRENGTHS OF THE WISHBONE

The strengths of the wishbone triple option series are as follows:

1. It is easy for the offensive line to learn, as the blocking rules are simple and fairly easy to execute.
2. Since the attack has numerous plays, it can be used as an entire offense.
3. Only the defenders inside of the offensive tackle have to be blocked.
4. The defenders outside the offensive tackle do not have to be forced or driven off the line of scrimmage.
5. The release of receivers from the line forces the secondary to back pedal or retreat, and perhaps causes them to revert to zone coverage.
6. Maximum speed is utilized along the line of scrimmage.
7. Three backs located in the backfield are excellent for various fakes, power, and diversion.
8. The fullback thrusts straight ahead on most plays, adding constant pressure to the defense.
9. The faking and deception occur along the line of scrimmage and not deep in the backfield.
10. Usually the best and most powerful back is utilized to run the ball up the middle.
11. Average personnel can easily be employed with the entire series. Brute force and power, etc., are not necessary.
12. Counters, reverses, and other options are simple to incorporate.

13. Play action passes are facilitated by the fact that the receivers are continually releasing from the line of scrimmage on every play.

14. Any wrong move or slight positional mistake by the defense can be easily exploited.

WISHBONE ERRORS

Such a finely-tuned system is susceptible to many errors. If the quarterback and fullback do not coordinate, or if the trailing halfback is not in a suitable position, fumbles and other mistakes can occur and the entire offense may collapse. Since fundamentals, techniques, and timing are so essential, the offense requires a lot of patient drilling. In fact it may require a full season or more to properly develop the quarterback and the backfield.

A number of coaches contend that a successful triple option must be used as an entire offense to eliminate errors. So much time is involved in teaching technique, acquiring finesse and timing, that a team cannot be burdened with other plays and series. In short, a coach must go all the way with it. While this may be true, it is certainly not always the case.

WISHBONE PERSONNEL

The most important position is quarterback. The quarterback must learn the defenses in detail. He must know which players to read and key and how to react to the adjustments, blitzes, stunts, etc., of every defense. He also must be able to run the football. When forced to keep, he must cut hard upfield and react to the tacklers. And he should be rugged and tough to withstand the punishment he is sure to receive. Even though the triple option is basically a running offense, the quarterback must have the ability to pass. If he cannot, the defense can play the running game tight and tough.

The fullback who is going to run the ball a great deal should be a good hard-nosed ball carrier, as he's going to be tackled many times, even when he doesn't get the ball. Speed is essential. He must move quickly to the line and, once past it, should have the quickness and running ability to out-maneuver the defenders. The halfbacks who will do the blocking should be strong and hard-nosed to take on the bigger defensive ends and corner backs. They also must have enough speed to take the pitch and run outside. The pass receivers should have some talent for catching the ball, but they don't have to be exceptional blockers on the line of scrimmage. This is especially true of the tight end, who releases from the line. He should, however, be able to block downfield. The interior linemen don't have to be tough, big, or strong. The tackles just seal the defenders to the inside; they don't have to drive bigger and stronger opponents back off the line. The guards and center must stay with their counterparts and screen them from the play. Though it isn't necessary to drive these men off the line, the attack will be that much better if this can be done.

WISHBONE STRATEGY

It is essential that the quarterback be prepared mentally when attacking defenses. He should be taught the categories and characteristics of the seven-man front, eight-man front, and the unbalanced defense. He should have a knowledge of the count-off system of defenses and the basic responsibilities of each defender before or after stunts. The quarterback can better attack his opponent by having a complete knowledge of defensive play with its various stunts and what it tries to accomplish to stop the wishbone.

OFFENSIVE LINE SPLITS

Proper splits along the line are essential. Usually the fundamental split between each lineman is three feet. This can vary, however, according to the defensive set, play executed, and the characteristics of the opponents. *Diagram 6-5* indicates the splits for the offensive line.

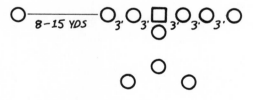

Diagram 6-5

WISHBONE BACKFIELD TECHNIQUES

The techniques and fundamentals of the four offensive backs are taught, practiced, and drilled so the backs work as one coordinated unit. Each step and movement must be well-timed. *Diagram 6-6* clearly illustrates the wishbone triple option play.

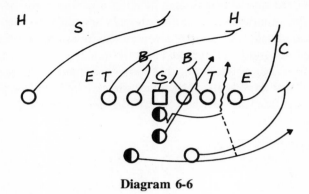

Diagram 6-6

The Quarterback

As the quarterback steps to the line he immediately scans the defense, establishing all his option and down-the-line keys before the ball is snapped. At the snap, he takes a 45 degree angled lead-step with the foot nearest the play. The ball is firmly in both hands and held at waist level. As this foot is planted, the body is in good alignment to mesh the ball into the stomach of the fullback who is driving forward for the guard-tackle seam. The ball is now placed into the pocket of the fullback. As the ball is being placed, the quarterback's eyes scan for his first initial key. It is a quick look, and the decision to give or keep the ball is realized during the ride of the fullback. The ball is kept in a plane parallel to the ground. An adjustment step now occurs as the fullback's momentum carries the quarterback's arms forward. As the ball travels toward the line of scrimmage, the next step is planted with the opposite foot near the neutral zone. This is a ride or adjustment step where the actual decision to present or withdraw the ball is attained. The weight transfers from the first to the second step. These two initial steps should not alter the course or path of the fullback. The quarterback, at all times, flows with the fullback and allows him ample room to run his course.

Within this split-second of riding time, a decision to either deliver or withdraw the ball is made by the quarterback. If the first key does not slant toward the fullback, the quarterback reacts by placing firm pressure with the ball into the belly of the fullback with the opposite hand. The fullback now holds the ball and drives for yardage upfield.

If the defensive action forces the quarterback to withdraw the ball, however, he immediately pushes from his second step, sets slightly deeper in the backfield, and runs toward his next option assignment. This is the "second level" of the triple option. His option technique at the defensive end, at this point, has already been explained. *Diagram 6-7* illustrates the footwork of the quarterback. *Diagram 6-8* shows the quarterback's first and second level of the option attack.

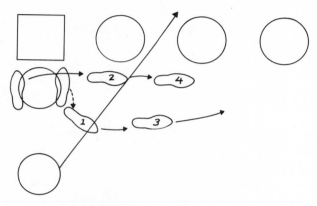

Quarterback's Footwork

Diagram 6-7

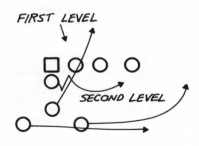

Diagram 6-8

First and second levels of the quarterback's path.

The Fullback

The fullback is always aligned directly behind the quarterback with his heels four yards from the ball. Most wishbone coaches desire a four point stance for the fullback. At the snap, the fullback initiates a lead-step with the foot nearest the play action and aims for the guard-tackle gap. This must be a constant step. Explosion and speed to the line are essential. Timing with the quarterback is also important. If the fullback is somewhat slower than the play actually requires, the coach should adjust him slightly forward in his alignment.

The fullback immediately forms a pocket with both arms ready to receive the ball. As the second step is completed, the quarterback has already arrived and offered the ball. A soft hold or pressure is placed on the ball and the fullback continues on his path. Once pressure is felt (done by the quarterback), he clamps down on the ball and continues forward for yardage. If the ball is withdrawn, the fullback continues on his designated course and blocks any linebackers or secondary as he maneuvers upfield. *Diagram 6-9* illustrates the footwork of the fullback.

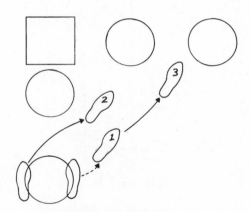

The Fullback's Footwork

Diagram 6-9

The Blocking Back

The offensive back nearest the designation of the play is the blocking back. From a wishbone standpoint he is located directly behind the offensive guard with his feet five yards from the line. He can be set in a two or three point stance. At the snap, the halfback's assignment is to block the defender responsible for the flat area. His initial lead-step is parallel to the line of scrimmage. His hips open toward the sideline to place him on his proper course. He remains on this lateral path and begins to round the corner once he slips past the defensive end's position. His block can occur anywhere along this path. He approaches the opponent from the outside and aims his face through the defender's outside hip. Once contact is about to be made, the blocker explodes his inside shoulder through the outside one-third of the defender's body, i.e., through the outside hip and thigh area. This should be sufficient to knock the opponent from his feet. If it isn't the blocker can roll into him and force the defender to bring his hands down. This is enough time for the ball carrier to break in or out and clear past him.

A common problem that confronts the blocking halfback is the defender that crosses the line quickly and attempts to force the runner inside into pursuit. When this occurs, the halfback simply utilizes a reverse body block *(Diagram 6-10)* and forces the opponent outside. The ball carrier must react by stepping inside momentarily before regaining his outside course.

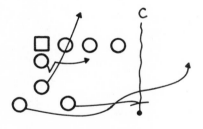

Diagram 6-10

The Trailing Halfback

The trail halfback aligns opposite his counterpart at the five yard depth. Once the ball is snapped, he pushes with his outside foot toward the play and runs the chalk line along the same path of the blocking halfback. His objective is to achieve a good option-pitch relationship with the quarterback. He should not have a timing problem especially with the ride of the fullback into the line.

WISHBONE LINE TECHNIQUES

The line blocking rules and techniques are discussed in detail in Chapter 4. Blocking rule C is employed with the triple option attack.

Other blocking combinations and coaching points are explained also. The outside release technique, "cat" block, bump technique, and "get" block are also all essential to the wishbone.

The Load Block Principle

A not so familiar scheme with other series is the "load" block. Shown in *Diagram 6-11,* the purpose of this block is to create added pressure on the defensive end. He not only must contend with the quarterback whom he is responsible for, but he has to confront a blocker as well. The quarterback's first read remains the same. However, if he withdraws the ball, he will react and run off the block of his halfback. Once past the defensive end, his next option is the cornerback. He can keep or pitch from the defender's reactions.

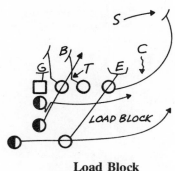

Load Block

Diagram 6-11

OTHER WISHBONE PLAYS

The Fullback Dive

A very simple play is the straight ahead dive with the employment of one-on-one blocking. From a defensive standpoint, it is viewed as the start of the triple option. *Diagram 6-12* illustrates the fullback dive. Blocking rule B, as described in Chapter 4, is utilized. However, since the play is definitely geared up the middle, the releasing end can aim toward the center of the field.

The Regular Option

The regular option *(Diagram 6-13)* can be employed instead of the triple option. Blocking rule B is used (Chapter 4). The fullback

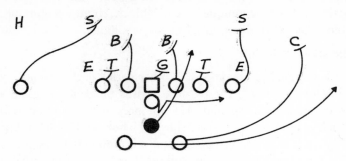

The Fullback Dive

Diagram 6-12

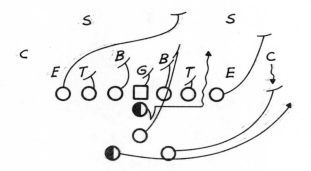

The Regular Option

Diagram 6-13

fakes through the guard area and blocks any defenders pursuing outside. The quarterback executes similar steps and techniques as the
triple option. However, the first read does not occur. He fakes to the
fullback and continues towards the defensive end.

The Counter Play

There are two counter dive plays an offense can use to strike.
Diagram 6-14 illustrates a counter with the fullback carrying the ball.
This is geared more for a two-back backfield than the wishbone set. At
the snap, the fullback jab steps (as if diving) in the opposite direction
of the counter. The next step, however, is not forward, but aimed

toward the center-guard seam on the opposite side of the center. He continues forward on this course, receives the football, and runs for daylight. The quarterback quickly reverse pivots and presents the ball to the fullback. He continues along the line to fake the counter option play. The tailback also jab steps in the same direction of the fullback. He pushes away, however, and begins the counter option course.

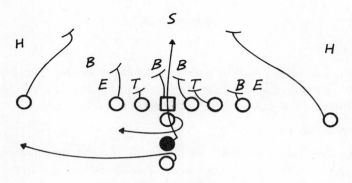

Diagram 6-14

The second counter and more popular one is shown in *Diagram 6-15*. The quarterback reverse pivots. He open-steps as if he is going to ride the fullback. The second step is brought next and parallel to the first one. He turns on this foot and executes the reverse pivot. Once he spins around, he is facing in the opposite direction and is prepared to hand the ball to the diving halfback. As the ball is delivered, he continues along the line and fakes the counter option at the defensive end.

The fullback can perform one of two maneuvers. First, he can fake a regular dive play (as shown). Secondly, however, he can jab step, reverse his course, and sprint in the opposite direction parallel to the line of scrimmage on his normal counter option. The ball carrier (diving halfback) lead-steps forward at a 45 degree angle with his inside foot. He then explodes forward, keying the first down defensive lineman to the side of the play. His aiming point is the center-guard gap. Once the ball is handed to him, he continues forward and seeks

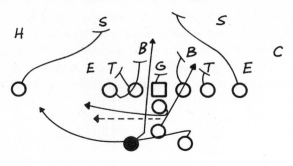

Diagram 6-15

daylight. The offside halfback also jabs, but pivots and sprints on his counter option course. Blocking for both the inside counter plays can vary. Either a one-on-one or a fold (cross) can be applied.

The Quarterback Counter

An excellent quarterback counter play is illustrated in *Diagram 6-16*. The entire backfield flows in one direction creating quick defensive pursuit. The quarterback fakes to the fullback, but veers in the opposite direction through the center-guard area.

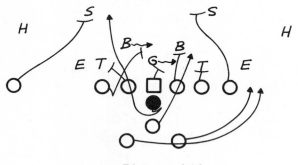

Diagram 6-16

The Counter Option

One of the best offensive plays geared for any quick flowing defense is the counter option. It has excellent thrust, both toward the field and the sideline because of the counter dive fake tending to freeze defenders near the middle area. The quarterback partially fakes to the counter halfback dive and continues toward the defensive end. The fullback jab steps away from the actual direction of the play, pivots, and sprints back running parallel to the line. He is responsible for the defender aligned in the flat defensive area. The trailing halfback jab steps also and follows behind the fullback. He should achieve a good option-pitch relationship with the quarterback. The end, whether set tight or split wide, drives from the line and is assigned the deep outside one-third of the field. Blocking rule B is used as described in Chapter 4. *Diagram 6-17* illustrates the counter option.

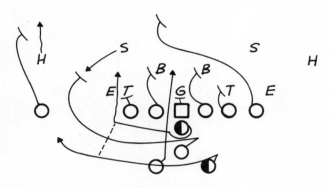

The Counter Option
Diagram 6-17

The Quick Pass

To take intelligent and strategical advantage of quick secondary support, the wishbone series can use the play action pass as a strong offensive weapon. One of the first passes introduced is the quick short pass to either the tight or split end. The quarterback ride fakes the dive fullback. Once the fullback clears the area, the quarterback quickly rises tall, sets, and hits the tight end releasing straight upfield. It is an excellent pass, whether facing quick defensive invert or rotational coverage *(Diagram 6-18)*. A similar play action pass can be accomplished toward the split end as well.

Diagram 6-19 illustrates a counter pass from the fullback fake. Again, once the fullback clears, the quarterback quickly steps back-

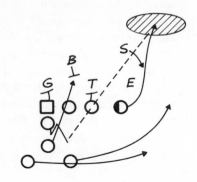

Diagram 6-18

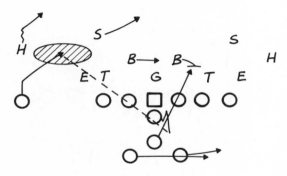

Diagram 6-19

wards and throws in the opposite direction. When linebackers flow quickly to the fake, this becomes an excellent play.

The Counter-Option Run or Pass

The counter-option run or pass is a tremendous play that should be drilled repeatedly. The ball is either thrown to the releasing receiver or the quarterback options the defensive end as shown in *Diagram 6-20*. After the quarterback reverse pivots, initiates a good fake of the counter dive, he immediately scans and reads the tight end. If the end is clear, the quarterback instantly passes the ball to him. However, if he is well covered, the quarterback continues along the line at the defensive end and options him. This is a delicate play where practice and patience is accentuated. If the option portion isn't desired, the counter-pass can still be executed by itself.

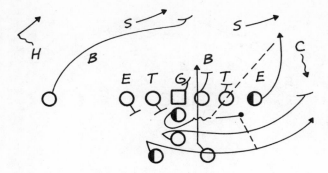

The Counter-Option Run or Pass

Diagram 6-20

Set-Up Play Action Passes

There are instances when the quarterback sets up to throw deeper patterns due to down and distance, score, field position, etc. Actions in the backfield can either be observed straight or counter. Of course, the pass patterns chosen are strategically geared to defeat the coverage of the secondary. *Diagrams 6-21 through 6-23* serve as examples of various actions and patterns that can be utilized. In Diagram 6-21 the split end executes a curl route while the halfback dashes to the flat. The fake of the fullback should freeze linebackers momentarily so a clear alley or opening to the split end is created. Diagram 6-22 illustrates the fake of a counter dive with a square-out route. Diagram 6-23 is another counter fake and a clearing pattern is used.

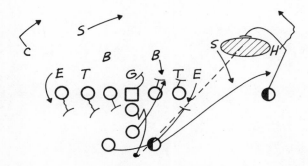

Diagram 6-21

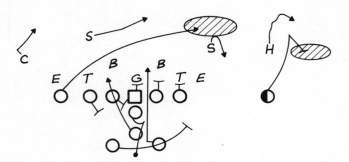

Diagram 6-22

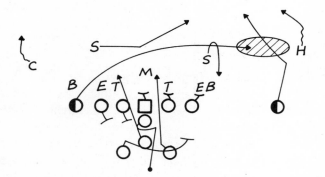

Diagram 6-23

7

THE VEER TRIPLE OPTION

The veer is another concept in the exciting triple option threat. While the triple option itself plays an important role, there are other aspects to the attack the offense can capitalize upon. The veer has a diversity of formations. It has actually more than the wishbone. While the wishbone accepts the three-back power theory with the blocking halfbacks, the veer mobilizes both the run and pass. The formations are geared to spread the defense. By accomplishing this, with the promise of the passing game, the veer has a better opportunity to succeed and grind out yardage on the ground.

OBJECTIVES OF THE VEER

The veer has other distinct advantages over the wishbone. Since it spreads the defense, it is a wide-open attack. Passing becomes essential. If the offense can threaten the defense in the secondary zones, the deep defenders cannot react forward quite as fast to the running game. They must be careful. A wrong move forward to stop the run, at an inappropriate time, could result in a pass completion or even a touchdown.

The offense also relies on quick and speedy halfbacks. While the wishbone required speed, blocking backs were also necessary. Not so with the veer. Speed is essential with good outside running ability. However, the backs do not have to block quite as effectively. The veer is also a finesse attack. A large measure of time and energy is spent on the fine and exact details of out-maneuvering the defense. Blocking, power, and brute force are just not necessary.

TRIPLE OPTION SIMILARITIES

As mentioned with the wishbone, the veer remains very similar in attack capabilities. It is a goal line to goal line offense. The same plays can be used up and down the field. It is a balanced offense. Identical plays executed towards the tight end can be used to the split end. The play and execution are alike. The parallel is true with a majority of the passing attack. From week to week the game plan remains constant. The same formations and plays remain part of the attack. Some, but not many, new wrinkles are always added. The veer is an easy and an uncomplicated offense. Because of the nature of the triple option, time and drilling are necessary to achieve perfection. However, the various plays and blocking assignments are rather simplified. Of course the blocking or the option itself may change slightly, but the fundamental attack remains the same.

STRENGTHS OF THE VEER

Other than what has been already mentioned, the strength of the triple option weapon remains virtually identical to that which was described in Chapter 6.

FAVORITE FORMATIONS

The two veer formations widely used are either the two-wide outs located to either side of the center or positioned only on one side. *Diagram 7-1* illustrates these formations (pro or twin).

THE INSIDE VEER TRIPLE OPTION

Diagram 7-2 illustrates the execution and blocking assignments of the inside veer triple option.

QUARTERBACK TECHNIQUES

At the snap of the ball the quarterback brings the ball to his waistline with the elbows resting against his hips. As the ball is

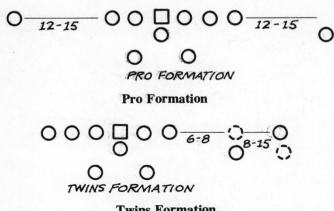

PRO FORMATION

Pro Formation

TWINS FORMATION

Twins Formation

Diagram 7-1

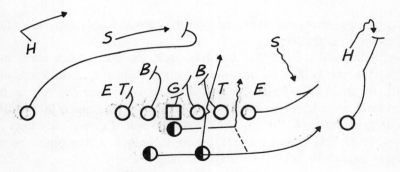

The Inside Veer Triple Option

Diagram 7-2

brought up, his first step is along and slightly into the line *(Diagram 7-3)*. He immediately scans for his first key, whether to hand-off or keep the ball. The arms extend slightly to offer the ball to the dive halfback. As the next step is completed the decision to give or not is made. If the defender remains stationary, reacts out, or crosses the line, the ball is delivered to the diving halfback. The quarterback's hand nearest the line slides the ball firmly into the pocket so the halfback can grasp it easily. However, if the defender slants inside aiming for the dive man, the quarterback simply pushes from his

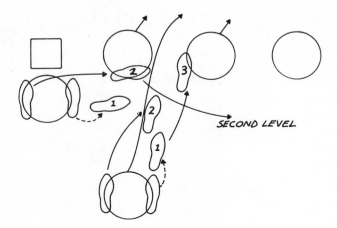

Diagram 7-3

second step, starts his movement on the second level, and views the next option defender.

If the ball is handed to the dive back, the quarterback continues along the line to fake the next option action. However, if he keeps the ball, he attacks the defensive end quickly, but under control, as he descends upon him. As described in Chapter 2, the quick toss to the trailing halfback can be applied. Since the ball is continually kept at waist level, this is an excellent tossing technique. Other option techniques explained in Chapter 2 can be taught also.

DIVE HALFBACK TECHNIQUES

The preferable stance of the dive halfback is the three point with the hand nearest the option (right hand if going right) extended for balance. The halfback's heels should be from 4 to 4½ yards in depth from the line and directly behind that of the offensive guard's. This distance and width from the center will vary according to the speed and timing between the quarterback and diving back. The dive back's first step is with his outside foot. His aiming point is through the outside foot of the offensive guard. He continues thrusting forward with as much speed as possible. Once this first step is completed, he automatically forms a pocket and prepares to receive the ball if the read for the quarterback shows. Once into the line and the ball delivered to him, the halfback should veer slightly outside and away from any pursuit sliding from the inside. If the ball is not given, he still continues to remain on this same course so he can block any quick defenders. A good fake, however, should be executed if the ball is not delivered.

TRAILING HALFBACK'S TECHNIQUES

The trailing halfback's stance and alignment are similar to the diving halfback. At the snap, the halfback pushes from his outside foot and travels a path that aims through the feet of the dive back. He darts at full speed so he is in proper position to receive the pitch from the quarterback after the dive back has cleared into the line. Since the quarterback faces various stunts, the pitch may be delivered quickly. Therefore, the back must be fully prepared for a quick toss.

THE FLANKER BACK

The wide-out back, when executed from a pro formation, is assigned the perimeter as described in Chapter 5. The various adjustments are indicated also.

OFFENSIVE LINE BLOCKING

Chapter 4 illustrated and explained in detail the blocking assignments. Blocking rule C is the principal blocking scheme. Other combinations are indicated such as the outside release technique, cat block, bump technique, etc.

THE OUTSIDE VEER TRIPLE OPTION

Another triple option interlaced with the veer series is directed at the off-tackle seam. Known as the outside veer triple option, the dive back's path is aimed through the off-tackle hole. *Diagram 7-4* illustrates the outside veer.

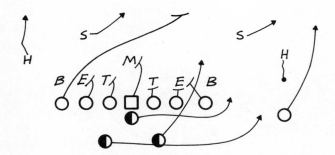

The Outside Veer Triple Option

Diagram 7-4

IMPORTANT COACHING POINTS

This play can only be geared to the seven-man front defense such as the 5-4, Pro-4, various stacks, etc. A double team blocking combination must be attained at the off-tackle hole. This cannot be achieved against eight-man alignments. Another essential principle is that the outside veer play be directed towards a tight end. The end and the adjacent tackle are the double team blockers.

QUARTERBACK TECHNIQUES

The quarterback's initial steps, after taking the snap, are identical to that of the inside veer. However, he must now travel with extreme quickness along the line, for the ball handling procedures occur at the off-tackle area. As he accelerates, he scans immediately to the defender located just outside the offensive end's position. If this man (most likely the defensive end) slants inside for the dive back, the quarterback retains the ball and turns upfield. His next key is the defensive halfback. The defensive secondary coverage can either be an invert zone, rotational zone, or strictly man-to-man. If the invert occurs, the quarterback can either maintain or pitch the ball from the defensive reaction. However, if the defense utilizes rotational coverage, the quarterback will probably cradle the ball and swerve upfield. He should gain excellent yardage if this occurs *(Diagram 7-5)*. With man-to-man coverage, the defenders are constantly back pedaling and yardage should be achieved also.

If the defensive end reacts out, remains in his original alignment,

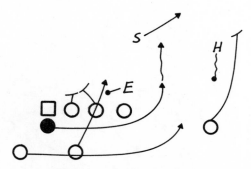

Rotation and the Outside Veer

Diagram 7-5

or crosses the line of scrimmage, the ball is handed to the dive back. The ball should be presented with the inside hand nearest the line of scrimmage (if going right it is with the left hand). The ball is firmly placed into the pocket which is created by the dive halfback. Slight pressure can be applied so the back can feel and easily handle it. Once the ball is delivered, the quarterback continues upfield and fakes the option-pitch to the trailing halfback.

THE HALFBACK DIVE TECHNIQUE

Two slightly different methods can be taught the halfback on his dive techniques. His aiming point is through the outside leg of the offensive tackle. If the halfback is slower than the quarterback and arrives late at the mesh juncture, his first step should be immediately directed toward the off-tackle hole as indicated in *Diagram 7-6*. He continues forward on a direct path. Once he reaches the hand-off area a pocket is formed for the quarterback. If the ball is given to him, he promptly slants outside and away from the pursuit. However, if the ball is not delivered he remains on his course, glances inside, and knocks down any defender (usually linebackers) pursuing from that direction.

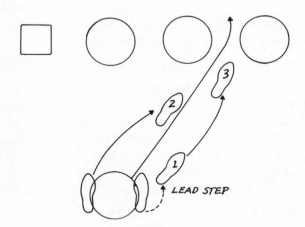

LEAD STEP

Diagram 7-6

The second technique *(Diagram 7-7)* is used for a faster halfback or if the quarterback cannot reach the hand-off point in time. The dive halfback's first step is forward with the inside foot. His next step,

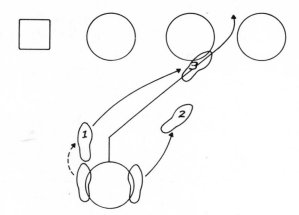

Diagram 7-7

however, is directed to the aiming point. His assignment and responsibilities remain identical to that of the first technique mentioned.

THE TRAIL HALFBACK'S TECHNIQUES

The trail halfback's path is identical to that of the inside veer. He sprints through the original alignment of his counterpart and maintains a good option-pitch relationship with the quarterback.

OFFENSIVE LINE BLOCKING

Blocking rule A is used exclusively for the outside veer play. This was described in Chapter 4. Either a double team block is executed or a bump technique can be added against the linebacker. It is essential that any inside linebackers be sealed inside as much as possible. A good seal (standing tall and walling the linebacker) or chopping him is the best. Blocking at the perimeter, whether it be one wide-out or two wide-outs aligned to one side, is described and illustrated in Chapter 5.

COUNTERING DIFFICULT STUNTS

The stunting game can result in many mishaps if the offense is not fully prepared. Film and game study is a necessity. An example of one difficult stunt to block and read is indicated in *Diagram 7-8*. Constantly viewing films can assist both the quarterback and the tight end. As the tight end reads the slant, he slams the defensive end inside, but slips upfield to wall the linebacker inside. The dive halfback remains

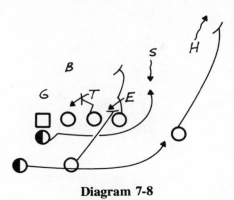

Diagram 7-8

low and blocks the defensive end. The quarterback retains the ball with
the read and swings into the defensive secondary. All the defensive
pursuit should be secured inside.

THE STRAIGHT DIVE AND SINGLE OPTION

For simplicity, without reading the triple option, the offense can
utilize the straight ahead dive utilizing one-on-one blocking. Blocking
rule B explained in Chapter 4 is applied. The quarterback simply hands
the ball to the dive back with the ball carrier scanning and thrusting for
daylight *(Diagram 7-9)*.

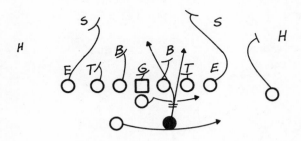

The Straight Dive

Diagram 7-9

Similar blocking can be employed with the single option
(Diagram 7-10). The quarterback fakes the delivery to the diving halfback. The halfback continues through the line and blocks any defen-

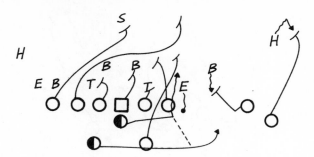

The Veer Single Option

Diagram 7-10

ders charging outside. To either keep or pitch the ball to the trailing back, the quarterback continues along the line at the defensive end.

THE COUNTER DIVE

One of the first counters used by the veer offense is the counter dive illustrated in *Diagram 7-11*. The ball carrier (in this case the left halfback) establishes a quick jab step as if starting on his normal trailing position. Once the step is completed, however, he swings and aims through the center's foot to his side and keys the first down lineman on that side. He veers to one side or the other according to the success of the block. If facing a 5-4 Defense, the ball carrier reads the middle guard. If it is a Split 4-4, the halfback keys the defensive tackle.

The quarterback steps in the opposite direction of the play as if he is beginning the triple option. However, with one quick motion, the

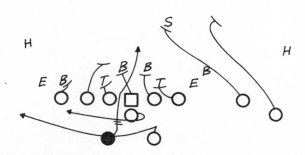

Diagram 7-11

second step is shortened and is placed parallel to the first. This is a pivot step also. The quarterback spins completely around to hand the ball to the counter dive halfback. Once the ball is delivered, the quarterback continues along the line to fake the counter option play.

The remaining halfback steps forward with the outside foot as if he is aiming to dive forward. However, he pivots and crosses the center to fake the counter-option with the quarterback. His path brings him through the original alignment of the ball carrier. The offensive line utilizes one-on-one blocking. A fold block shown in *Diagram 7-12* can be used also.

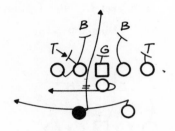

Diagram 7-12

THE COUNTER-OPTION

The counter-option is one sequence resulting from the counter dive. The quarterback, dive halfback and trailing halfback execute identical steps as described with the counter-dive play. The quarterback continues along the line to the defensive end after faking the hand-off to the diving halfback. It is of the utmost importance that as soon as the quarterback reverse pivots he is fully prepared to pitch the football. This is especially apparent towards a split end where any defender can attack the quarterback by stunting or slanting inside from the corners. The quarterback, therefore, must be prepared to pitch the football immediately once he has completed the fake.

Blocking rule B described in Chapter 4 is used. *Diagram 7-13* indicates the counter-option play.

THE CON VEER

Another excellent dive action is the con veer. This can be executed when defensive linebackers and linemen pursue quickly outside. *Diagram 7-14* illustrates the con dive versus the 5-4 defense. As can be

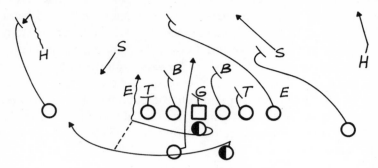

The Veer Counter Option

Diagram 7-13

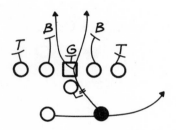

The Veer Con Dive

Diagram 7-14

seen, it is directed at the middle guard. The dive halfback simply accelerates and aims through the defender. The quarterback steps back, opens his hips, and presents the ball to the halfback. He should allow the ball carrier plenty of room to run. The blocking used is one-on-one.

THE VEER CON OPTION

Another variation of the counter option is a con option originating from the con dive play. As shown in *Diagram 7-15* the quarterback reverse pivots, fakes to the dive back, and continues along the line for the option. The opposite halfback, instead of darting across the center, cruises with the quarterback for the pitch. This is an excellent play because the halfback is already in proper position for the toss. His speed should be controlled so that he maintains an accurate relationship

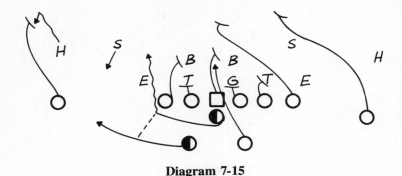

Diagram 7-15

with the quarterback. Rule B remains the blocking scheme for the con option play.

THE VEER PASSING GAME

For any veer offense to be successful it requires a sound passing game. Unlike the wishbone attack, the veer can only survive on the premise that if the defense converges on the run, the offense will pass. If the defense disperses for the pass, the offense will strike on the ground. The offense, of course, can utilize the entire passing game, i.e., the dropback, sprint-out, and sprintback, along with the play action looks illustrated throughout this chapter.

The veer pass can be categorized into four different areas.

1. The Straight Action Pass
2. The Counter Pass
3. The Sprint Pass
4. The Dropback Pass

The Straight Action Passes

Once the defensive linebackers and secondary are focusing on the run, it is time to pass the ball. One of the first passes to execute is the tight end. This is an excellent pass play, especially versus a three deep zone or four deep rotational coverage. If the defense inverts quickly to the option run, the tight end or second receiver positioned from the outside-in has a good chance to become clear also.

Diagram 7-16 illustrates a simple fake dive to the halfback. The

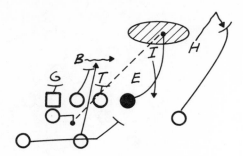

Diagram 7-16

frontside line aggressively attacks the defense, while the backside protects inside and drops for pass protection. The tight end releases to his
outside, aiming for as much width as possible before swinging for
depth. Once the defensive end has been cleared, the receiver dips
upfield, avoiding any linebackers inside. The receiver should never
drift inside, for if he does, interceptions can occur. The outside receiver (flanker, split end) releases as if it were an option. Once the ball
is thrown, he breaks into a good football position and blocks the
defensive halfback. Some schools of thought have the wide-out execute a route (square-out) as an outlet receiver.

The same play action in the backfield is indicated in *Diagram
7-17*, but toward the split end. This route is good when the secondary
rotates forward. If rotation does not occur, other routes can be designed such as the quick out, slant, curl, hook, square-in, etc. Many
schools read the secondary *after* the snap with the route being determined by the coverage.

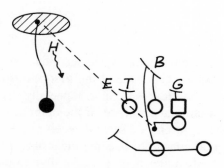

Diagram 7-17

Other formations can be utilized also. A two wide-out formation located toward one side of the center is an example. Whether the defense rotates or inverts the inside receiver should be clear. Of course man-to-man coverage can be used, but the effectiveness of the defense converging to the run diminishes. *Diagram 7-18* illustrates this pass toward a twins' formation.

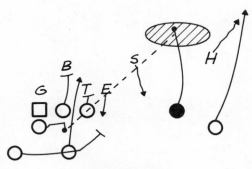

Diagram 7-18

The Counter Passes

Faking the counter dive and throwing to various patterns are other options. The counter play action freezes linebackers more and there is less chance of an interception by the inside linebackers. *Diagrams 7-19 through 7-21* illustrate various patterns from the action of the counter dive. In Diagram 7-19 the quarterback sets for the tight end. While not shown, the identical pass can be applied toward a twins' formation.

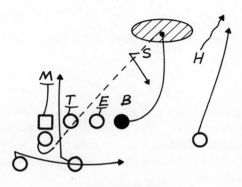

Diagram 7-19

Diagram 7-20 illustrates the counter to a split end. The receiver darts on a short post. Diagram 7-21 shows a similar route to a twins' set. The split end spurts for seven steps and bends inside on a post route. The inside receiver aims outside and swings up the sideline. The quarterback has the choice of passing to the quick post or hitting the sideline route.

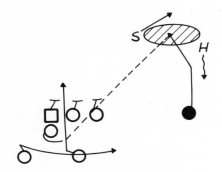

Diagram 7-20

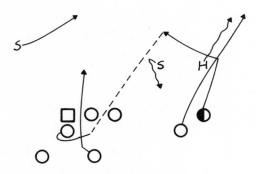

Diagram 7-21

The Sprint Passes

The sprint pass can be executed once a fake to the dive halfback is completed. The quarterback steps along the line, quickly fakes to the halfback, and then accelerates on an arc path behind the blocking of the trail halfback. The frontside blocking is aggressive, while the backside uses dropback pass techniques.

Any pass pattern can be executed to the side of the play action. *Diagram 7-22* illustrates a simple square-out by the flanker and a short flag route by the inside receiver. The blocking halfback plunges across the center's plain and collapses the defensive end inside. The quarterback rolls outside the block and automatically peers for the square-out. If the defensive halfback is aligned adjacent to the receiver, the flag should be clear. A hook pattern from a twins' formation is indicated in *Diagram 7-23*. The inside receiver can decelerate between the defensive halfback and safety in the open area.

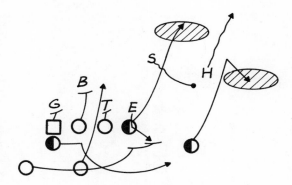

The Square-Out

Diagram 7-22

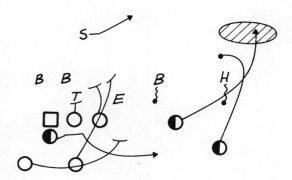

The Hook Route

Diagram 7-23

The Dropback Pass

Faking to the dive halfback or counter dive creates numerous problems for the defense. The defenders must first respect the run. Second, the offense can capitalize on any number of pass patterns, since the quarterback is dropping and setting away from the line. Pocket protection is formed with the interior linemen. Pass patterns vary according to the secondary coverage, down and distance, field position, and score of the game. Two examples of setting back are portrayed in *Diagrams 7-24 and 7-25*.

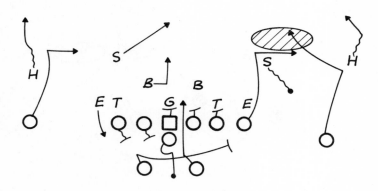

Diagram 7-24

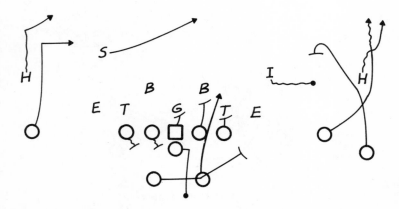

Diagram 7-25

Diagram 7-24 illustrates the wide receiver running a post while the tight end squares out. The quarterback fakes to the counter-dive halfback, drops to a position seven to nine yards behind the center, and glances quickly for the post route. If the post is covered, the square-out becomes the outlet. Diagram 7-25 illustrates the dive fake with the curl pattern exploited. In this case, the inside receiver spurts approximately five yards from the sideline and swings upfield. If he can defeat the defensive halfback or safety, he continues at full speed. If, however, the deep areas are well covered, the receiver quickly decelerates into the vulnerable area.

8

THE SWING OPTION

The swing option is one of the most uncomplicated, but most successful plays in football. Faking is not required anywhere along the line. All the quarterback needs to do is to take the snap from center, locate the defensive man he is to option, and attack him as quickly as possible. The purpose of the swing or speed option is to strike at the perimeter as quickly as possible. The play attempts to defeat pursuit outside. If the line can seal or wall off all defenders away from the area, the result will add to success. If the swing option can arrive at the corner rapidly, the quarterback or trail halfback has excellent opportunities to swing upfield unimpeded. The only blocks essential at the perimeter are by the fullback and another halfback or wide receiver *(Diagram 8-1)*.

FORMATIONS AND SPLITS

Field width is essential for the swing option. The formation can be set tight, but the option and blockers must quickly face two fast secondary support men as indicated in *Diagram 8-2*. Since backfield faking

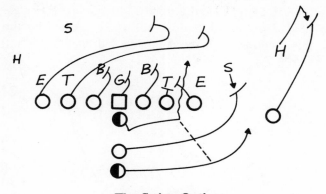

The Swing Option

Diagram 8-1

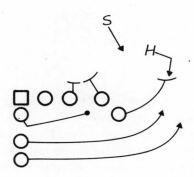

Diagram 8-2

Two defenders are in a better position to cover the swing option. They can read the swing easier, also.

does not occur, the defenders can quickly dash forward for the quarterback or pitch man. However, if the offense sets wide-outs (either one or two), the defensive secondary must compensate and spread out with them. The widest defender on the field is the defensive halfback and he is concerned with the pass first. When he does react for the contain or trail halfback, he is aligned too wide to disrupt the pitch quickly enough. This gives the ball carrier a better opportunity to gather himself, once he has the ball, and initiate any ball carrying maneuvers in the open field. *Diagram 8-3* illustrates width created by the flanker back and the relationship of the defensive halfback to the pitch.

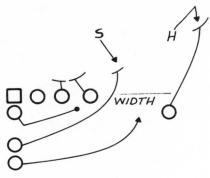

Diagram 8-3

As can be seen, width forces a defender back and away from the quarterback and receiver.

The best backfield alignment for the speed option is the ''I'' set. The trailing halfback is constantly in a good relationship with the quarterback to accelerate or decelerate. His instant depth and vision allow him to view the quarterback and corner area. If the halfback is aligned in almost any other position, he has to bolt in motion to achieve a favored pitch relationship with the quarterback. Faking does not occur in the backfield with the quarterback. Therefore, the trailing halfback does not have the opportunity to adjust his course or relationship with the quarterback when aligned in another location.

The blocker's strength at the tight end's position (or a halfback from a slot) is critical to the success of the play. His ability to block against various defensive schemes can set the tone for the kind of formations adopted by the offense. Against related seven-man fronts he can easily strike the defender aligned inside with his counterpart, the offensive tackle. However, when he faces certain eight-man fronts, the end is assigned the defender positioned over him. A one-on-one situation develops. If the tight end can manage this engagement, the offense can adopt any perimeter offensive alignment. If he can't, the offense should split him wide to achieve defensive adjustments advantageous for the offense. If the offense splits the end, a defender may align wider and deeper from the ball. Various blocking adjustments can now be exploited. If a defender doesn't cover the wide-out, the play will have to be automaticked.

The splits along the line should be normal without too much width. Fakes are not included inside, and the quarterback wishes to approach the option defender as quickly as possible. The line can even minimize its splits to assist the play.

QUARTERBACK TECHNIQUES OF THE SWING OPTION

When attacking the defensive end there are four distinct but successful footwork techniques.

1. The Lead Step
2. The Step Back and Crossover
3. The Step Back and Lead
4. The Drop Back and Set

The Lead Step

The lead step technique has the quarterback take the ball from center and open step along the line directly toward the defensive end *(Diagram 8-4)*. He doesn't attempt to attain any depth in the backfield whatsoever. Because of this method the halfback must be very quick, so he can accelerate ahead of the quarterback for the possible toss.

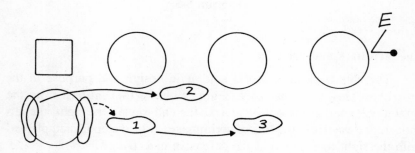

The Lead Step Technique

Diagram 8-4

The Step Back and Crossover

The step back and crossover is a more common technique. Once the ball is put into play, the quarterback steps straight back away from the center with the foot nearest the option defender (if the play action is right, the right foot is brought back). It is brought straight back, but when planted, aimed at the defender to be optioned. The next step (left) crosses in front of the first step. The purpose of this technique is to attain slight depth in the backfield so the quarterback can approach the defensive end at an angle that will take him into the line. His shoulders and entire body can turn inside the off-tackle area advantageously. His eyes scan the option area better also. At the same instance, it allows the halfback ample time to reach his proper pitch relationship with the quarterback. *Diagram 8-5* clearly illustrates the step back and crossover technique.

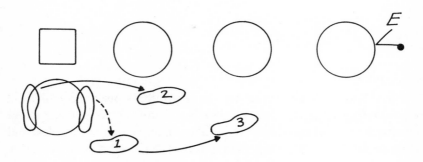

The Step Back and Crossover Technique

Diagram 8-5

The Step Back and Lead

The step back and lead is similar in design and purpose to the crossover. However, the stride begins with the foot farthest from the option defender. If the option attacks the end toward the right, the left foot steps away from the line of scrimmage. A lead step is then planted with the right foot aimed at the defensive end *(Diagram 8-6)*.

The Drop Back and Set

The drop back and set is an exceedingly delayed swing option technique. It is valuable for either one of three reasons. Many drop-

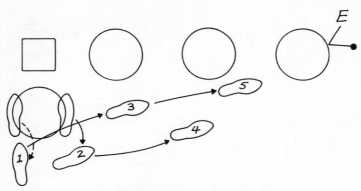

The Step Back and Lead Technique

Diagram 8-6

back passing teams execute this technique because the quarterback begins to drop simulating either the quick pass or the start of a drop-back pass. Secondly, an offensive back does not necessarily have to be aligned in an ''I'' set. The trailing halfback can now hustle across and behind the quarterback's position and maintain the proper relationship necessary for the pitch. Third, it tends to hold linebackers and other defenders for a moment. This assists the offensive lineman's block and helps to seal the defenders away from the perimeter. While these advantages are beneficial, it does slow the play considerably.

The first step is completed with the foot nearest the option defender. It is brought straight back and away from the line. The second is brought directly away also and planted parallel to the first. At this point the quarterback hesitates for a slight second to freeze linebackers and secondary defenders. The knees are slightly bent, hips down, head up, and ball held at the chest level. The quarterback now leads with the foot nearest the defender he is to option, while pushing from the opposite foot. After it is completed, the opposite foot crosses over in front and is aimed on the option course. *Diagram 8-7* indicates the drop and set technique.

FULLBACK TECHNIQUES OF THE SWING OPTION

The fullback is usually set directly behind the quarterback. Other offenses have positioned him either behind the guard or even wider. A midway point can be used also. These alignments are presented to offer

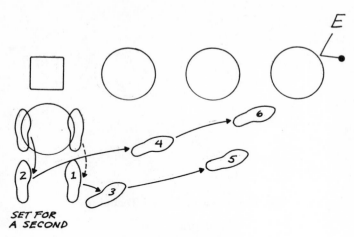

Diagram 8-7

good blocking relationships with the ball carrier. At the start, the fullback initiates a quick lead open step, moving parallel to the line of scrimmage toward the point of attack. He remains on this course until he is approximately one yard outside the original alignment of the tight end. His assignment is the defender responsible for the flat area of the secondary. This is either a defensive halfback rotating forward or an invert safety driving from the inside-out. *Diagram 8-8* illustrates his course and blocking responsibilities. A beneficial key for him is the invert safety. If the safety rushes forward, the fullback automatically blocks him inside. However, if he races to the deep outside one-third of the secondary, the fullback's target now becomes the defensive halfback.

In both cases, the fullback's intended point of attack is the outside hip of the defender. He aims for that portion of the defender with his head continually in an up-level position. He should never take his eyes from his target. As the defender approaches, the fullback aims his inside shoulder at the outside hip. Once contact is imminent, the blocker drives solidly through the defender's hip, exploding with his shoulders, back, hips, and thighs into and through him. A crossbody block is now applied. This technique should knock the defensive man down. If he is still fighting to keep his feet, however, the blocker can roll into his legs attempting to keep him occupied. The ball carrier

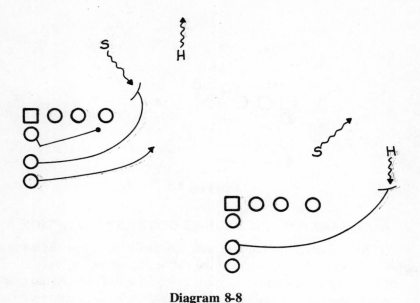

Diagram 8-8

(trailing halfback), who is running directly behind him, can now swerve in either direction and gain yardage upfield. Common fullback mistakes are to execute the block earlier than necessary, thereby missing the defender entirely, or to lower the head before contact is made.

There are instances when the defender flies forward so quickly that the fullback doesn't have the opportunity to reach the outside hip. A rather simplified coaching point is for the fullback to read color. As the blocker rounds the corner for his assignment and the defender crosses his vision more quickly than anticipated (the opposite colored jersey flashes across his face), he must adjust his blocking course and technique. He can no longer block the outside hip effectively. As the defender crosses in front of him, the fullback automatically and instinctively utilizes a reverse crossbody block through the inside hip of the defender. To apply this block, the fullback reverses his body and throws his inside hip into the air. He aims at the inside hip of the defender. A crossbody block, its techniques and rolling effect into the defender is still appropriate but thrust by the opposite hip *(Diagram 8-9)*. In this case, the ball carrier slips inside the block, but quickly escapes outside away from pursuit and into field space.

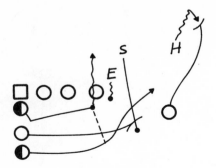

Diagram 8-9

BALL CARRYING TECHNIQUES OF THE SWING OPTION

There are three techniques that are available when the swing option is called. The alignment of the halfback from an "I" formation is approximately one-and-a-half yards behind the fullback. At the snap of the ball, the tailback lead-steps and aims outside. His second step is a cross-over *(Diagram 8-10)*. He continues on a course parallel to the line and maintains a good option-pitch relationship with the quarterback. This is an advantageous technique as long as the fullback has adequate speed to get outside the option defender and be removed from the pitch if it should occur.

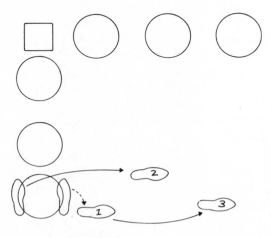

The Lead-Step

Diagram 8-10

The second technique is the drop-step and go. This technique allows the fullback the opportunity to slightly slip ahead of the ball carrier. Therefore, the relationship of the fullback (blocking) and half-back (running) is excellent. The halfback *(Diagram 8-11)* completes a backward or drop-step with the foot nearest the point of attack. This allows a moment for the fullback to clear both the quarterback and tailback. Once the first step is planted, the second becomes a cross-over in front of the first toward the direction of the play. The tailback now continues outside with the quarterback.

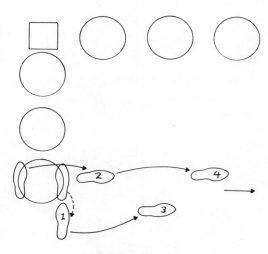

The Drop-Step

Diagram 8-11

The third is the counter step technique. At the snap of the ball, the halfback undertakes a jab step in the opposite direction of the intended path of the play. The purpose, of course, is to allow the blocker an ample chance to get in front of the ball carrier. The following steps maintain a proper relationship with the halfback on his course with the quarterback *(Diagram 8-12)*.

BLOCKING COMBINATIONS

Blocking rule A, described in Chapter 4, is the scheme most applied to the speed option. Perimeter blocking is specifically explained in Chapter 5. The widest receiver blocks the outside one-third

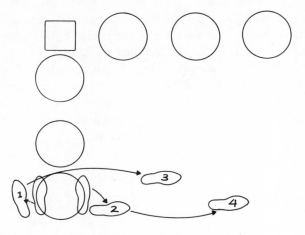

The Counter Step

Diagram 8-12

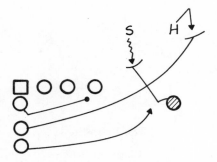

A Quick Block on the Invert Safety

Diagram 8-13

of the field with the fullback responsible for the defender assigned to
the flat. A crossing combination can be adopted with the swing option
also. *Diagram 8-13* illustrates the wide-out and fullback switching
assignments. The main purpose for such a change is because of the
fullback. He may have difficulty in executing his block mainly because
the invert safety is flying up fast attempting to disrupt the option in the
offensive backfield.

Bump Block

If an offense is successful with the speed option, many defenses widen their linebackers. They allow them to quickly react outside as soon as the option action is observed. If the linebacker cannot be sealed inside, the speed option may not succeed. If this occurs, the offense can apply the bump block. Two different techniques can be utilized. Instead of the tight end double teaming the defensive tackle inside, he lead jab steps inside at a 45 degree angle. His shoulders remain parallel to the line of scrimmage and his body action is low. The following step is dispatched straight upfield. He now peers for the linebacker inside. Two defensive reactions can occur when using this technique. First, the defensive tackle could loop wide outside toward the end on a stunt or slant charge. Since the offensive tackle blocks him alone, the end should assist the tackle by double teaming. Second, if a stunt does not occur, the tight end continues upfield and aims through the outside hip of the linebacker. He knocks the linebacker down by driving his inside shoulder through the hip and thigh and eventually rolling into his legs. However, the tight end can aim slightly higher through the numbers and shield or wall the defender from the outside. *Diagram 8-14* illustrates the steps executed to reach the linebacker while *Diagram 8-15* shows the various defensive reactions and the needed blocking. The quarterback should be aware of this block, since he should pitch the ball and not swing upfield with it himself.

The second technique is similar to the first, except the tight end never considers the defensive tackle's charge. If the defensive tackle loops outside he is completely disregarded, with the end blocking the linebacker. When this technique is executed, the end does not introduce quite a jab step inside. The movement is upfield through the

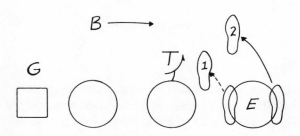

Diagram 8-14

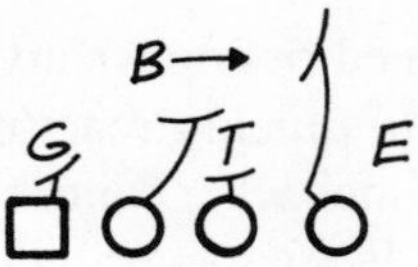

Straight Defense 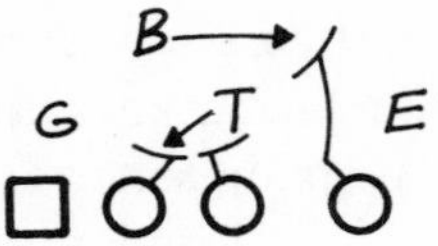   Tackle Slants In

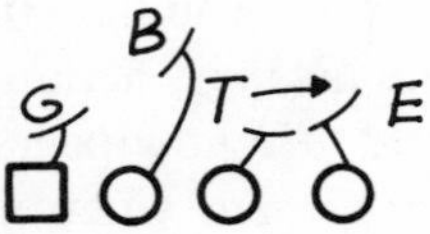

Tackle Loops Out

Diagram 8-15

inside shoulder of the defender aligned over him. He escapes all personnel and blocks only the linebacker. The offensive tackle's assignment is to handle the defensive man over him alone. To accomplish
this, his first step aims him slightly wider than the defender's alignment. If the defensive man remains straight or loops out, the tackle has
a good angle to block him. If, however, the tackle slants inside, the
guard traps his penetration while the tackle scoops upfield to add
assistance to the tight end *(Diagram 8-16)*.

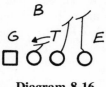

Diagram 8-16

The Scoop Block

While the bump technique can be geared toward most seven-man
front defenses, the scoop block is only effective versus the 5-4 or a variation of it. The scoop block's purpose is not only to seal the linebacker
inside, as accomplished with the bump, but to double team the defen-

sive tackle as well. It is not as difficult a block as it may first appear to be. The split between the guard and tackle is substantially reduced as much as possible. Once the play begins, the guard aims along the line and attempts to block the far (outside) knee of the defensive tackle. The guard's only responsibility is to prevent any penetration across the line of scrimmage. The offensive tackle launches a similar first step aimed outside. His responsibility is to deter any looping action of the defender. If a loop charge does not occur, the tackle can now swing inside and shield him from the hole. If the block is executed correctly the linebacker and defensive tackle should be completely obstructed from the option. The quarterback and halfback can still carry the ball (the quarterback could not maintain the ball with the bump block). The only real disadvantage of the scoop technique is the chance of a linebacker stunting through the guard-tackle seam. Of course when linebackers are aligned deeper and wider there shouldn't be a possibility for this to occur.

Two Wide-Out Formations

As discussed at the start of this chapter, formations can dictate defensive alignments that are advantageous to the offense. When linebackers cannot be halted outside or a tight end has difficulty with a one-on-one situation, the offense should adjust to a two wide-out formation. When this is presented, a defender must cover the flat area or be subjected to the passing game. *Diagram 8-17* illustrates a twins' formation with the speed option utilized. Notice the inside wide receiver slants inside and sets for a linebacker, while the fullback's responsibility is the outside defender.

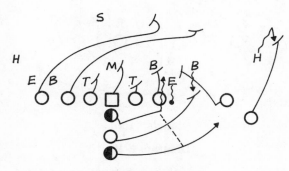

Diagram 8-17

One of the distinct advantages of the two wide-outs is their ability to communicate with each other and, therefore, block the secondary according to its coverage. In many cases, the secondary cannot disguise its coverage because of the alignment of the twins' formation. The two receivers can add certain words that signal the scheme necessary for the particular coverage. Three examples are indicated in *Diagrams 8-18 through 8-20.*

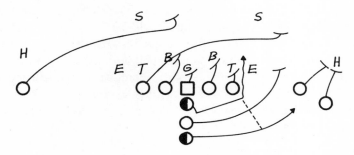

"Double" Call

Diagram 8-18

The inside receiver calls "double" because of the quick rotation shown by the defense.

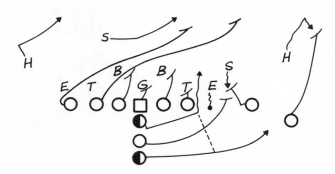

"Single" Call

Diagram 8-19

The inside receiver notices an invert coverage and utters a "single" call. He blocks the flat while his partner is assigned the deep outside one-third.

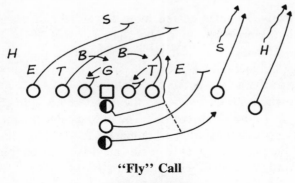

"Fly" Call

Diagram 8-20

The inside receiver automatically reads man-to-man coverage and delivers a ''fly'' call to the outside man. At the snap, both men accelerate downfield drawing the defenders with them.

THE FULLBACK AS THE BALL CARRIER

If the fullback has quickness and is a swift ball carrier, he can carry the ball from the speed option. In this case, any formation can be used. However, he must be aligned either behind the quarterback or adjusted slightly over toward the play side. The normally optioned tailback can now align either in an ''I'' or anywhere else. Since he is needed as a blocker in front of the fullback, motion is used *(Diagram 8-21).*

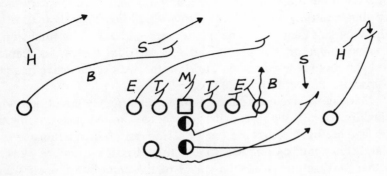

Diagram 8-21

THE COUNTER-OPTION

An effective counter geared more toward the sideline than the open field is the counter-option play. The purpose of the counter is hopefully to slowdown linebacker and secondary pursuit. The line must sustain its blocks since faking doesn't occur, and it is somewhat delayed due to the action in the backfield.

As shown in *Diagram 8-22,* the quarterback quickly reverse pivots and attacks the defensive end. The fullback departs immediately to his blocking assignment. The tailback jab steps in the opposite direction of the play, but quickly begins his drive outside remaining in a good option-pitch course with the quarterback.

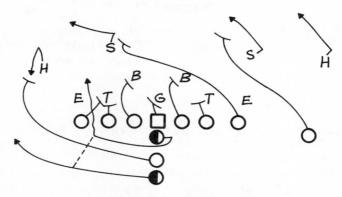

Diagram 8-22

SWING OPTION PLAYS

There are only a few plays that can be administered from the swing option action. An efficient running counter is the quarterback keep illustrated in *Diagram 8-23.* Both backs flow outside, expecting to draw pursuit their way. The quarterback initiates his normal step in the same direction, but pivots and reverses into the offside center-guard gap. Fold blocking is used to abort the nearest defensive linemen (in this case the defensive tackle).

Many defensive teams attempt to prevent momentum of the swing option by forcing their secondary coverage around and driving the defensive halfback across the line of scrimmage. When defensive secondaries react quickly and accomplish this, then it is absolutely essential that play action passes be called to the appropriate open areas.

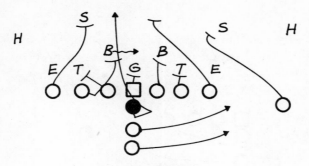

Diagram 8-23

Diagram 8-24 illustrates the quarterback maneuvering along the line as if optioning the defensive end. However, he sets back and behind his tackle with any appropriate pattern being adopted. The diagram pictures a squareout route with the tight end feigning inside and darting to the flat as an outlet receiver.

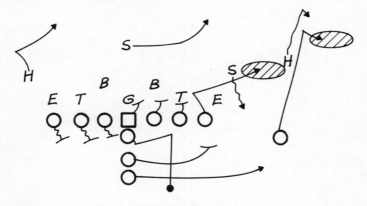

Diagram 8-24

An excellent play action pass, however, is introducing the halfback as the passer. The quarterback travels toward the defensive end *(Diagram 8-25)* as if to option him. Once in proximity, however, the quarterback flips the ball to the trailing halfback. This action usually draws the defenders forward for the run. The halfback now sets (or runs) and passes to the open receiver. Again, any pass pattern can be used in order to exploit the weaknesses created by the defensive actions.

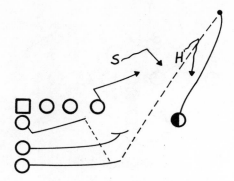

Diagram 8-25

9

THE OUTSIDE BELLY
OPTION

FORMATION REQUIREMENTS

The outside belly series is usually geared toward a tight end. The angle and path of the fullback require fundamental and sound blocking at the off-tackle area. The fullback is normally aligned behind the quarterback. Other halfbacks can be located anywhere. One halfback, however, must be placed so he has the opportunity to become a trailing option-pitch ball carrier. A few coaches require a halfback to block in proximity to the running hole. This creates a situation where the offense has to adopt some version of the straight T formation or a three back offense. *Diagram 9-1* illustrates the formation and path of the fullback.

THEORY OF THE OUTSIDE BELLY OPTION

The belly play concept is to isolate a defender on the line of scrimmage and allow him to react in either direction. When the ball is

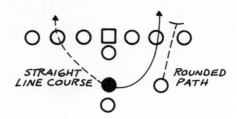

The Outside Belly Path

Diagram 9-1

handed to the fullback, he can beeline to either gap and run to daylight. It compounds pressure on the defensive end also. The end has to be drilled and disciplined to occupy and control his ground. In half the cases the ball (when the option itself is called) is withdrawn from the pocket of the fullback and brought to the secondary where additional running pressure is exerted upon the defenders.

THE OUTSIDE BELLY TECHNIQUES AND ACTION

The Fullback

While *Diagram 9-1* indicated the path of the fullback, the actual techniques to get to the line can vary. Aiming points change also. However, there are numerous similarities and the two fundamental methods are illustrated.

The most common fullback path is an arc route aimed at the inside leg of the offensive tackle. On the snap, the fullback initiates a short lateral step directed outside with a full crossover stride made with the second step. He remains parallel to the line, with the body leaning forward and low to the ground. A pocket is formed for the quarterback as the second step is taken. On the third stride, the fullback begins to gain ground upfield and slants his path for the inside leg of the tackle.

As these steps are generated, the fullback takes notice of the tackle's block. The shoulders continually remain parallel to the line. This allows the fullback, once he has the ball, to swerve right or left as he enters the neutral zone. If the shoulders are turned outward, even slightly, the fullback has a decreased opportunity to glance inside for any openings.

As the second and third steps are made, the quarterback has met him and situated the ball into the pocket created by the fullback. The ball carrier clamps onto the ball as the quarterback "rides" him for a step toward the line. During this time, the fullback should be concentrating on the blocking scheme of the offensive line. Stunts and blitzes should be read so the fullback can seek daylight as he moves. Once the fullback crosses the line it becomes essential that he scan for openings, but at the same instant, accelerate upfield for the goal line. The fullback runs at full speed, for he will have to bowl over defenders at times to gain the necessary yardage. A linebacker should never prevent his forward progress. Constant drilling is a must so this doesn't occur. *Diagram 9-2* illustrates the fullback's footwork.

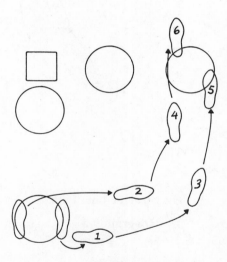

The Arcing Path of the Fullback

Diagram 9-2

Another current belly course is directing the fullback on a straight line toward his offensive tackle. Because of the quicker speed to the line (the path has been reduced), the unbent path is adopted by some coaches. At the snap of the ball, the fullback commences a short lateral step as mentioned previously. However, on the second stride the fullback aims directly upfield toward the inside leg of the tackle gaining ground. The third step follows suit. The fullback continues along this path until he reaches the original alignment of the offensive tackle. At this point the fullback strives to swing his shoulders upfield and parallel to the line so he has the opportunity to look in either direction for daylight. As the second step is planted, the arms form a pocket for the ball. At the same time, he remains low to the ground so he can scoot quickly if an occasion presents itself. *Diagram 9-3* illustrates the straight path and aiming point of the fullback.

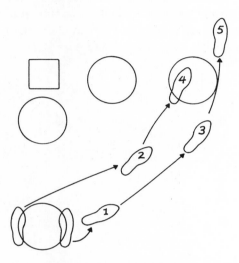

The Straight Line Path

Diagram 9-3

The Quarterback Techniques

The quarterback, also, has two different methods he can apply to execute the outside belly play. One method is the direct open-out action aimed toward the fullback action. While being the first used course, it is still widely accepted today. From a good stance the quarterback open-steps with the foot nearest the play action at a 45 degree angle. This step is directed away from the line and into the backfield. It is essential that this first step, from its start to its completion, gain ground backwards and at the correct angle. If the quarterback is too shallow or deep he will not mesh properly with the fullback. The ball is held at waist level with the elbows slightly bent and swaying with the hips. With the next two steps, the quarterback meshes with the full-back. This backfield juncture is approximately two or three yards in depth. As the third step is planted, the opposite foot is brought parallel and pointed toward the offensive tackle. The quarterback rides the fullback at this point toward the line. The weight of the body is shifted from the back to the forward foot. The ball is released to the fullback once the hands and arms arrive at a point close to the quarterback's inside hip. The quarterback's position remains low with the hips down, knees bent, and head up. With his body weight placed on the inside foot, the quarterback pushes away and aims toward the defensive end to fake the option. *Diagram 9-4* illustrates the quarterback's footwork.

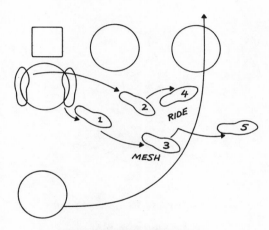

The Open Step Technique

Diagram 9-4

Another common method used in the belly play is the reverse pivot technique by the quarterback. From a good stance under the center, the quarterback pushes away from the foot nearest the flow of the play. The quarterback's weight is placed on this foot because he is swinging to pivot on it. The ball is brought to the belt line with the quarterback rolling two-thirds around and aimed at a 45 degree angle away from the line of scrimmage. As this first step is planted, the quarterback immediately glances for the fullback and then scans toward the line and the defensive end. A second step is followed at the identical backfield angle away from the line. As this foot hits the ground, the mesh and ride begins with the fullback. As can be seen, the quarterback completed only two steps to reach the mesh point, rather than the three steps for the open technique. It is essential with the reverse pivot that the quarterback quickly snap his head toward the mesh and the line of scrimmage. Since he is reversing away from the line, he is momentarily blinded from the entire action and play. Because of this, he must expedite his movement to compensate for it. *Diagram 9-5* indicates the quarterback's reverse pivot footwork.

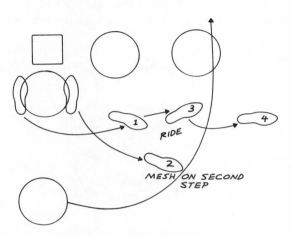

The Reverse Pivot Technique

Diagram 9-5

Blocking Techniques and Strategy

Line blocking schemes are rather simple. Blocking rule A and its combinations are described in Chapter 4. There are two exceptions, however. The onside end's rule changes. He now blocks "On-Out." Within rule A, he either blocked the defender aligned on him or drove inside to double team with his offensive tackle. However, on the normal give to the fullback, he blocks out on the defender located outside him (defensive end). The tackle's block alters slightly also. His technique depends upon whether or not he receives assistance from an offensive halfback.

If the halfback isn't set to block (flanked wide as an example), the tackle attacks the defender by himself. He blocks through the numbers and drives him wherever he lunges. This is an extremely difficult block, since the offensive tackle must wield the man whether he plays normal, slants inside, or scoops outside. As long as he can maintain contact and not lose him or drop to the ground, the fullback has the opportunity to break away from the defender *(Diagram 9-6)*.

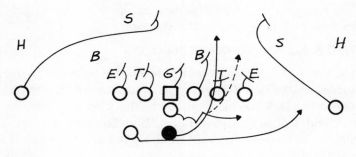

Diagram 9-6

If the halfback is in position to block (a normal halfback alignment), the tackle can strike the defensive man through the inside numbers. If the defensive tackle plays straight or slants out, the tackle and halfback double team him. The halfback drives from his alignment and aims through the outside portion of the defender. If the defensive man slants in, the tackle blocks him on his own (the inside aiming point helps considerably), and the halfback continues upfield scanning for any linebacker pressure. *Diagram 9-7* illustrates the blocking versus the 5-4 and Split-4 defenses.

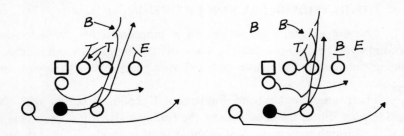

Diagram 9-7

The Trailing Halfback

The trailing halfback on the option play can be located in any position. He can be set in an I, normal set, or at a wing or slot alignment. When situated wide, he must fly back in automatic motion in order to maintain his relationship with the quarterback. At the snap of the ball, the trail halfback completes a deep open step in the direction of the action and sprints at full speed to the option-pitch area. Since the ride with the fullback is delayed, he may have to decelerate his speed once he is in position for the toss.

OTHER BLOCKING COMBINATIONS

There are other means by which the outside belly can be executed and blocked on the line. *Diagram 9-8* illustrates both a trap block by the guard and a kick-out block by the halfback on the defensive end. The backfield actions remain identical. Both blocks versus the defensive end should be executed with an inside-out approach aimed at the inside hip of the defender.

Diagram 9-8

THE OUTSIDE BELLY SINGLE OPTION

The outside belly single option is pinpointed for the defensive secondary. The fullback fake is made off-tackle with the quarterback racing outside the defensive end and swinging upfield to option the secondary personnel.

There are two key and fundamental coaching points with the option play. First, the coach steers the fullback slightly wider. This is usually through the outside leg of the offensive tackle. This may only be a two-foot variance, but it can forestall the defensive end and allow

the quarterback enough time to dart past him. Second, if the fullback is
taught the straight line approach, he should not utilize the first lateral
step previously described. His first step aims directly toward the
outside foot of the tackle, and he sprints for the hole.

The defensive ends can be left alone when they are reacting inside
and tackling the fullback. If this occurs, the offensive halfback can
flank wide to create defensive width and spreading. Blocking rule B is
adapted *(Diagram 9-9)* with a variation shown in *Diagram 9-10*. With
the offensive end blocking inside on the defender, the defensive end
should react even more inside.

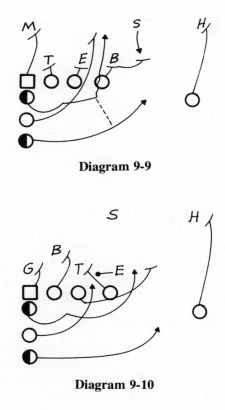

Diagram 9-9

Diagram 9-10

The defensive end will have to be blocked when he is disregarding
the fullback. This is usually accomplished from a wing position as
shown in *Diagram 9-11*. Identical techniques and blocks are main-

tained. However, the offensive end walls off the linebacker inside, the fullback seals the defensive tackle, and the wingback collapses the defensive end. If the defensive end reacts inside, the wing continues upfield for inside pursuit. The quarterback fakes to the fullback, drives past the wing's block, and turns upfield.

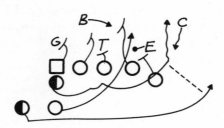

Diagram 9-11

The Quarterback's Shuffle Technique

Another quarterback technique may be added at this point, since the fullback's course is wider. When the open-out technique is practiced, along with the straight line path of the fullback, the mesh point between both of them will be quicker. If this materializes, a quick shuffle step is sufficient.

As the quarterback open-steps (when to the right it is with the right foot) toward the fullback, his next movement is to quickly push from the right foot, land quickly gaining little ground with the left. The third step or right foot is brought forward to mesh with the fullback. The quarterback now rides with the fullback toward the outside leg of the offensive tackle. *Diagram 9-12* illustrates the footwork.

THE BELLY TRIPLE OPTION

An exciting play that has caused numerous headaches to defenders is the outside belly triple option. Various techniques can be used by both the fullback and quarterback. The reverse pivot or open-out technique can be applied initially. It is essential, however, that the quarterback look immediately at the defensive end once the ball has been snapped. This is vitally important with the reverse pivot. As the quarterback rolls out, he immediately swings his head around and scans the off-tackle area. A stunt may develop quickly which he should automat-

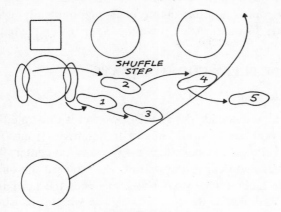

Diagram 9-12

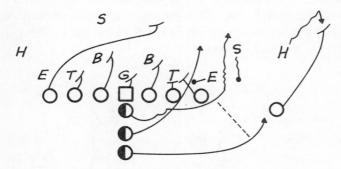

The Outside Belly Triple Option

Diagram 9-13

ically recognize and react accordingly. The fullback can apply either the direct (straight line technique) or the curved path approach.

Diagram 9-13 illustrates the belly triple option. Blocking rule A is used. Perimeter blocking is explained in Chapter 5. The quarterback reverses and rides the fullback while reading the defensive end's reactions. If the end remains in his original position, or sets across the line, the fullback is given the ball. If, however, the defensive end slants inside, or reacts in to the movement of the tight end, the ball is withdrawn. The quarterback races past the defensive end and immediately swings upfield toward the defensive secondary. If the coverage is rotational, the quarterback automatically maintains the ball. If invert, the quarterback can either keep or flip the ball to the trail halfback.

OUTSIDE BELLY COUNTER PLAYS

The Halfback Trap

A trap aimed outside the guard's position is illustrated in *Diagram 9-14* versus both an eight and nine man defensive front. The quarterback either reverses or open steps away from the center. The fake by the fullback is identical to the option, i.e., toward the outside hip of the offensive tackle. The quarterback executes the normal ride sequence. Once completed, the quarterback has weight distributed on the forward foot. To facilitate the hand-off, the quarterback pivots back toward the ball carrier and delivers the ball with the hand that during the ride fake was farthest from the line. In other words, if the play's action is directed left, the ball is presented with the left hand and with the right hand when the action is right. Once the ball is given, the quarterback continues outside.

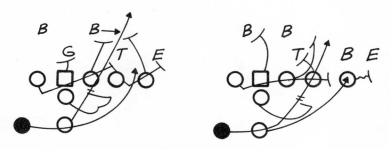

The Halfback Trap

Diagram 9-14

The ball carrier begins his normal trailing course with an open lead and crossover step. On the third, the halfback plants and aims behind the pulling guard near the offensive tackle area. A pocket is formed for the ball and, once received, the halfback swerves upfield for the open areas.

The Quick Counter Trap

Another excellent quick trap can be coordinated with the belly action also. Not only is it fast, but has counter-action which creates pursuit problems for the defense. The quarterback simply reverse pivots quickly and hands directly to the onside halfback slanting over the center *(Diagram 9-15)*. The halfback's course is straight without any delay. At the snap, he aims for the center area and reads the guard's trap block. The opening will vary according to the type of defense. The fullback and remaining halfback execute their normal fake and trail-pitch relationship with the quarterback. The line applies quick trap blocking.

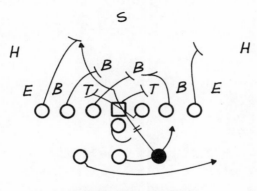

A Quick Counter Trap

Diagram 9-15

The Counter Draw

A counter draw running play is executed from the belly pass *(Diagram 9-16)*. The linemen toward the fake of the backfield use aggressive blocking. This shows run because of their drive action at the defense. The linemen away from the belly action, however, set to pass. This draws the defenders toward the hole, but also forces linebackers to play soft, be less aggressive, and possibly flow backward for pass coverage. The backfield action is clearly belly action. A counter half-back, however, that can derive from a wing, slot, or his normal half-back alignment, delays slightly, drives outside past the fake of the fullback, and accepts the ball from the quarterback. He now runs for daylight. The running lane exists from the center outside to the end's position. The quarterback simply fakes to the fullback and hands back to the delaying halfback.

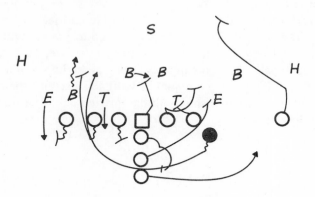

The Counter Draw
Diagram 9-16

The Belly Reverse

A reverse from the belly action can be called at times due to the defensive over pursuit. This is necessary when linebackers are flowing quickly to the ball's action. A reverse is not difficult to execute, but timing between the line and ball-carrier is important. *Diagram 9-17* illustrates a simple reverse play. The offensive linemen to the hole side block for a count or two and allow their defenders to release for pursuit. The onside end releases downfield as if the play were the belly. Once he is approximately seven to eight yards downfield, he peels back toward the sideline and forms a wall for the ball carrier. The onside tackle stalls for one count (this is the only position to do so) and quickly wheels around for the defensive contain man. Whoever the contain man is, i.e., defensive end or tackle, the blocker should be in position to chop him immediately as the defender reacts to the reverse. His relative position with the defender, therefore, is approximately one-by-two. In other words, he is one yard behind the defender in backfield depth and two yards outside him. He is now in excellent position to block him as the defender turns back for the reversing ball carrier.

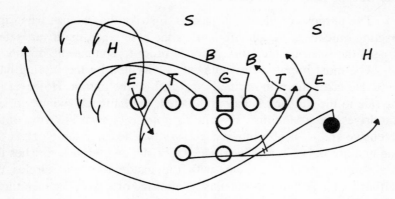

The Belly Reverse

Diagram 9-17

The onside guard, center, and backside guard hold their assignments for two counts, release toward the sideline, and form a wall along with the onside end. The backside tackle and end block for two or three counts before releasing. Penetration cannot be allowed along this area because of the delaying fake and the hand-off to the ball carrier.

The quarterback runs his normal backfield action. Once he is midway through the ride, he withdraws the ball and hands back to the ball carrier. The receiving wingback delays for two counts before scurrying back for the ball. The ball carrier can ensue from other alignments, i.e., flanker, twins, etc., but proper timing must be drilled. As he gathers the ball, however, he must gain depth into the backfield. He should be totally prepared to attain more depth if the defensive contain man quickly notices the reverse. If the ball carrier can maintain a distance from the defender, the offensive tackle has a good chance to use a crossbody block as he turns up and/or out for the halfback.

OUTSIDE BELLY PASSING PLAYS

There are two passing actions that can threaten the defense. Faking the belly and sprinting outside the defensive end or dropping backwards and throwing various patterns can be done.

The Outside Belly Sprint Pass

The purpose of the sprint pass is to strike the defense when it is reacting quickly to the option. This is the case when the invert safety crosses the line or stunts the corner in order to contain the option.

The most important assignment is executed by the trailing half-back. He takes the path normally traveled on the option. However, as the ride to the fullback is half completed, the halfback swings upfield and drives toward the line. His aiming point is one yard in front of the defensive end. It is absolutely necessary that he force the block at the line and not delay in the backfield. Once the quarterback finishes the ride action, he pushes away with the inside foot and circles the halfback's block to travel outside. The onside offensive linemen thrust off the line into aggressive blocks while the offside use pass protection techniques *(Diagram 9-18 and 9-19)*.

Various pass patterns can be perfected. The diagrams illustrate wing and a flank formation. In Diagram 9-18, the tight end feigns a block for two counts before darting in the flat. The wing automatically releases upfield to the flag. As he sprints, he reads the defensive coverage. Since rotation is usually used against a wing alignment, his route is geared between the safety and rotating halfback. Diagram 9-19 illustrates the curl route with the tight end aiming to the flat immediately. The curl receiver slides in either direction, but preferably outside and away from the underneath coverage.

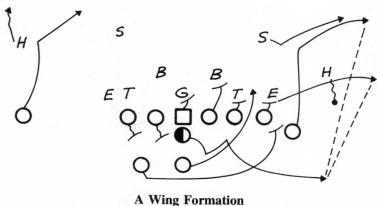

A Wing Formation

Diagram 9-18

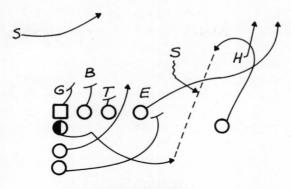

A Flank Formation

Diagram 9-19

Belly Dropback Action

A multitude of patterns, both toward the front and backside, can be employed with dropback action. *Diagram 9-20* illustrates one example of a dropback. After the fake is completed, the quarterback flies straight back and sets behind his offensive tackle. The halfback goes quickly for the defensive end. In this example, the split end accelerates on a post while the tight end crosses deep, about 18 yards, but in front of the deeper route. The safety valve is the flanker squaring-out. Aggressive, but controlled blocking is utilized by the onside linemen.

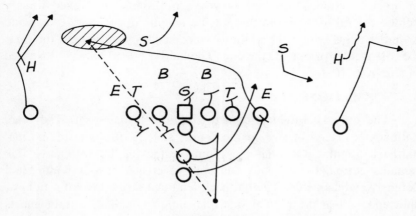

Diagram 9-20

10

THE LEAD TRIPLE OPTION

It is the I formation that brought the halfback lead play into the limelight. Other formations require two halfbacks to run with the ball in either direction. From the I, however, the tailback is aligned directly behind the fullback. From this set, he has the opportunity to execute different plays both right and left, whether they bear toward the middle, off-tackle, or outside the end. The halfback lead play is illustrated in *Diagram 10-1*.

FORMATIONS

The only backfield alignment required is the I set. The other halfback is placed in any position, i.e., slot, flank, or in his normal halfback alignment behind the offensive tackle. The offensive line remains normal or the ends can split to create various widths and defensive adjustments. The halfback lead can thrust toward a tight or split end. When the regular or triple option is called, a tight end is essential.

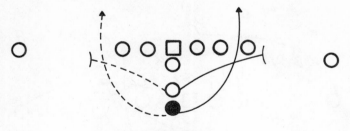

Diagram 10-1

THE LEAD OBJECTIVES

The actual run off-tackle is the fundamental play from the lead series. This play should be used as much as possible. As the lead becomes efficient and successful, the opportunity for the other plays to gain yardage and disrupt the defense naturally occurs. The many of-fenses that have established the series administer the lead thirty or forty times per game. Other plays are then implemented to force the defense off-balance.

There aren't many teams that have established the triple option theory with the lead play. However, it is an excellent way to option that can easily gain valuable yardage. The regular option can be of use also. In this case, a simulation of the lead is completed with a single option swinging upfield toward the defensive secondary.

PERSONNEL

While personnel is essential for any sequence of plays, the tail-back is the most important back on the field. If the lead is run often, the tailback must be a rugged, tough, but quick and agile ball carrier. Maneuverability in the line and scanning for daylight is a prerequisite. If this sequence is used heavily, it is sound for the offense to have a good back-up tailback should the number one tailback have to leave the game for any reason.

THE HALFBACK LEAD

Diagram 10-2 illustrates the lead directed to a tight end. There are different fundamentals and techniques taught with the lead play. The fundamental off-tackle play is mentioned first with the various options explained in succeeding pages.

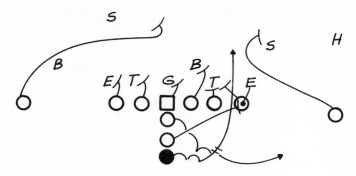

Diagram 10-2

Quarterback Techniques

There are two different techniques the quarterback can be taught with the halfback lead. The reverse pivot is the most common with the open-out technique used occasionally also.

The Reverse Pivot

At the snap of the ball, the quarterback reverse pivots out with the foot nearest the play action. All the weight is placed on the pivot. The opposite foot is swung around which lands at a 45 degree angle away from the line and toward the action of the lead halfback. The next step (second) is planted on the same angle from the line. The quarterback, at this point, meshes with the ball carrier who is aiming toward the off-tackle hole. The football is placed into the pocket of the tailback with the quarterback riding with him. The weight is now shifted from the second to the third step, which is short and directed to the line of scrimmage. The foot is planted with the toes aimed toward the running lane. As the ball rides forward, the quarterback releases it to the tailback. The ball is delivered as it reaches the inside hip of the quarterback. Once the ball is presented, the quarterback immediately brings both hands to the outside hip, pushes from his inside foot, and continues to reel outside past the defensive end. Forcing the halfback wide is a common mistake by the quarterback, for the hole may open inside. The hand-off should be smooth, with the quarterback swinging outside to fake and freeze the wide defenders. *Diagram 10-3* illustrates the reverse pivot's footwork.

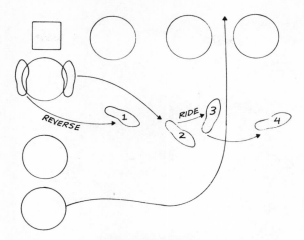

Diagram 10-3

The Open Step

A few coaches utilize the open-out method of approach. From a defensive standpoint it is observed as sprint-out action. At the snap of the ball, the quarterback pushes from the farthest foot. His hips open, leg swings out and around at an angle of 45 degrees away from the line of scrimmage. It is a lead step in the direction of the action. As this foot is planted, the second is completed at the same angle. Third step follows and is placed at the mesh juncture with the tailback. The ball is held at waist level during the entire flow. It is placed into the pocket formed by the tailback. Identical techniques required with the reverse pivot are applied through the ride and fake phase. *Diagram 10-4* illustrates the open step technique.

The Fullback

The fullback aligns in his normal position. His aiming point after the ball is put into play is toward the inside leg of the offensive tight end. At the start, a six-inch lead-step is initially made, and a direct line toward the off-tackle hole is established. While on the move, he reads the reactions of the defensive end. Various corner stunts should be anticipated which includes both linebackers and secondary. If the defensive end responds normally, the fullback aims his face and shoulder

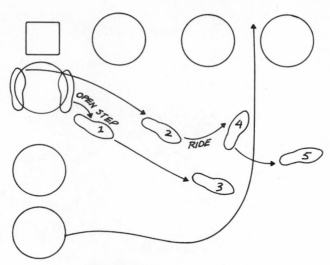

The Open-Step Technique

Diagram 10-4

through the defender's inside thigh. He explodes up and through the man forcing him outside. Powerful leg drive is important. Once contact is established, the legs continue to pound with the shoulders, back, and head driving forward and up. One of the fullback's greatest mistakes is leaving his feet in the hole. This is due to either not fulfilling a good block or falling to the ground. The tailback, now, not only reads daylight and swerves away from defenders, but has to avoid the fullback's legs as well. *Diagram 10-5* indicates the inside-out approach at the defensive end.

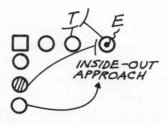

Diagram 10-5

Off-tackle stunts can create problems. Both the line and fullback adjust and modify their courses and blocking techniques to respond to the defensive movement. *Diagram 10-6* illustrates two simple stunts the fullback can observe while approaching the defensive end. In one case, the defensive end slants in front of the offensive end. The end automatically blocks him and the fullback knocks the linebacker out. In the second diagram, a defensive safety darts inside with the end looping outside. The fullback reacts and slams the safety outside.

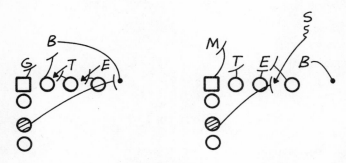

Diagram 10-6

The Tailback

The tailback's alignment behind the fullback is approximately 1 to 1½ yards. There are two courses or techniques the tailback can adopt. They are either the arc route or the direct path approach.

1. The Arc Route

The more common path for the tailback is the arc approach. The ball carrier begins from a two point stance. He leads and open-steps out. A crossover in front of the first follows. The stride itself and the shoulders remain parallel to the line of scrimmage. The tailback plunges forward on the third step and aims directly for the off-tackle hole. Automatically he allows his inside arm to form a pocket for the ball delivery. The quarterback meshes with the ball carrier at about the fourth or fifth step. The shoulders remain parallel to the line, the body leans forward slightly, and the eyes scan for the various blocking schemes. He is scooting at full speed with the ability to swerve in or out according to the openings and daylight. *Diagram 10-7* illustrates the tailback's footwork.

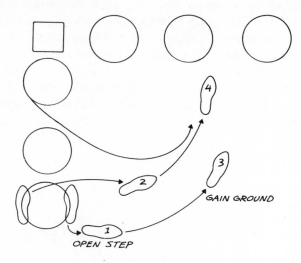

GAIN GROUND

OPEN STEP

Diagram 10-7

2. The Direct Path

A second method is a straight-line approach for the off-tackle area. After the first open-lead step is initiated, the tailback immediately gains ground with the second and thereon drives to the off-tackle hole. As he approaches the neutral zone, he attempts to turn his shoulders upfield. In this way he has the opportunity to seek a clearing both inside and outside. It is difficult for the tailback to break in if his shoulders and body don't swing upfield.

The Halfback

The remaining halfback can be set in any position to fake the option; however, he should be aligned away from the intended direction of the play. In this maneuver, he can accelerate around the hand-off point to take the option-pitch. The alignment varies from his regular halfback position to a slot or wing.

Offensive Line Blocking

The offensive line blocking scheme is rule A.

THE LEAD TRIPLE OPTION

The lead triple option is an excellent outside play that few teams attempt to install during a season. However, if an offense employs the lead off-tackle play the addition of the triple option has many benefits. With the style of reactions and stunts of defensive ends, it becomes increasingly more difficult to create openings at the off-tackle area. If, for example, the called play is the standard hand-off to the tailback, and the defensive end squeezes inside so an opening doesn't occur, the quarterback can't withdraw the ball and take it to the defensive secondary. If the triple option was included, additional yardage could have been gained if it were called.

Diagram 10-8 illustrates the lead triple option. The blocking scheme remains identical to the off-tackle play. As seen, there are unique differences with the techniques of the quarterback and fullback. The quarterback either reverse pivots or opens out, but his backfield depth is shallower to the line. The mesh and ride to the tailback become closer to the defensive end. This does not present, therefore, an opportunity for the defender to read whether the tailback is receiving the ball or whether the quarterback is withdrawing it. The fullback aims approximately one yard outside the defensive end. This path should draw the defensive man wide. If this occurs a definite give to the tailback is imminent. However, if the end reacts inside for the tailback, the quarterback withdraws the ball and continues for the next defender. The fullback proceeds outside and blocks the defensive corner back. As can be seen with the field space outside, a great deal of pressure is placed on the defender. He must not only remove the blocker, but also cover the quarterback's option of keep or pitch. It is the tailback's responsibility to fake having the ball and block the pursuit sliding from the inside.

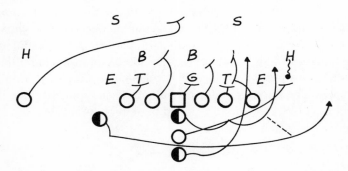

The Lead Triple Option

Diagram 10-8

Once the defensive end is exposed to the triple option he may attempt to outwit the offense by stunting or moving in one direction and reacting the other way. If the offense is concerned, the quarterback can consider the regular option. In this case, he automatically fakes to the tailback. The fullback's aiming point is similar to the triple option. As he approaches the end, however, he collapses on him and blocks through his outside leg. The quarterback naturally withdraws the ball and options the cornerback. Optioning the corner is simple even though he isn't blocked *(Diagram 10-9)*.

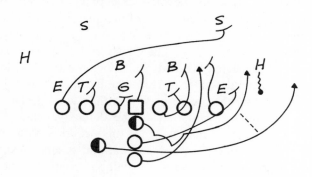

Diagram 10-9

THE LEAD PITCH

Another effective play isn't even an option. As *Diagram 10-10* illustrates, the bluff is completed with the tailback, but at the identical depth as the normal lead hand-off. The fullback aims directly at the corner, with the trail halfback sprinting outside the defensive end. As the quarterback withdraws the ball he takes one or two steps, and without optioning anyone, immediately pitches the ball out to the trailing halfback. This play is extremely effective, because drilling can be limited, an option is not considered, and the fullback blocks the cornerback. The feigning tailback seals the inside pursuit. The defensive end isn't blocked, but it is hoped he will be out of position for the trailing halfback due to the fake of the tailback.

THE QUARTERBACK KEEP

An inside fake, but a power running play outside the defensive end is the quarterback keeper. A trailing halfback isn't essential and he

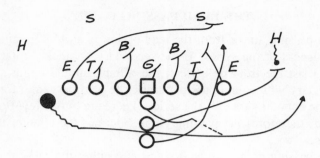

The Lead Pitch
(Automatic Motion Is Necessary
from the Wide Set)

Diagram 10-10

can be set anywhere. An offside guard pulls in front of the ball carrier
for added protection. *Diagram 10-11* illustrates the tailback fake. The
pulling guard drives from his alignment, slightly decelerates under
control where the lead is simulated, and then continues to sprint in
front of the ball carrying quarterback. It is essential the quarterback
gain slightly more depth once the ball is withdrawn to allow the guard
ample room to lead the play. The blocking along the line is aggressive.
The tight end can slip away from the double team and seal inside
pursuit. The fullback knocks the defensive end inside.

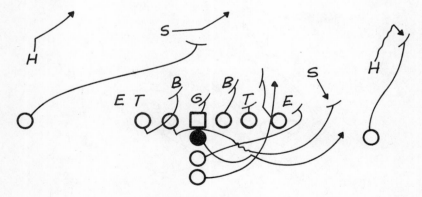

Diagram 10-11

THE LEAD PASSING GAME

The passing attack from the lead option is an important segment for the success of the series. If the secondary is quickly rotating forward to assist the front defenders, the offense should begin to attack the secondary with sound pass patterns. The passing game, for a large part, is the counter game for the series. There are only a few flow-back plays and, therefore, the passing game becomes the counter thrust of the series.

The passing game can be divided into either the roll-out or dropback action. Only a few patterns can be installed with the roll-out because the quarterback is dashing outside and usually can pass only to the frontside receivers. With the dropback, though, many various routes can be directed at the defense.

THE ROLL-OUT LEAD PASS

The roll-out lead pass can be havoc with any defensive end. The end must be prepared not only for the off-tackle run or option aspect, which he has to assist, but contain the roll-out action as well. *Diagram 10-12* illustrates the fundamental roll-out pass play. This pass and fake action is excellent versus any goal line defense also. The frontside linemen thrust aggressively as if the play were a run. The backside, however, drops away from the line for pass protection. The tailback aims off-tackle and pretends he has the ball. A good bluff is important. Not only do the down linemen hesitate, but if linebacker flow can be

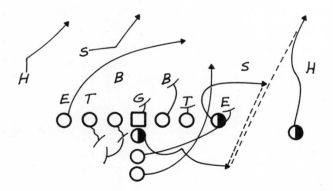

Diagram 10-12

slowed for a few seconds, the passing lanes should considerably widen. The fullback aims directly for the defensive end. At the last moment he explodes his inside shoulder through the outside thigh and hip of the defender. By keeping his head up and driving through, the end should be knocked down.

Simulating a block by the second inside receiver of the formation (in this case, the tight end) is essential. He blocks for one or two counts before releasing to the flat area. The widest receiver releases downfield inside, as if to block for the run, but quickly changes direction toward the flag. The backside end accelerates downfield immediately as if to crossfield block, but heads for the open areas.

As previously mentioned, the roll-out pass is excellent against any goal line defense. Since the defensive halfbacks and safeties are aligned two yards from the line, they are usually subjected and pressured to the fake. The defensive end must collapse to the run also. With the fullback's block made considerably easier, the quarterback reels out and usually has the choice of running or passing.

THE DROPBACK LEAD PASS

To drop away from the fake and set behind the blocking of the onside offensive guard and tackle is advantageous also. First, defensive linemen and linebackers are usually pressed to the fake. Second, three receivers can quickly release immediately from the line for an infinite number of passes. Third, the quarterback can set and scan in any direction according to the pass called. And fourth, either the tailback or fullback can sneak into the pass lanes as an added feature.

The blocking by the onside linemen is aggressive, but controlled. If a blocker is covered by a linebacker, he first checks the defender before assisting elsewhere along the line. The backside linemen pass protect away from the line as described previously. The fake of the tailback is similar to the roll-out. The fullback aims and aggressively attacks the defensive end as stated before. He remains controlled once contact is established. The quarterback simply reverse pivots, pretends to give the ball, and drops straight back approximately eight to nine yards. Any variety of patterns can be applied. *Diagrams 10-13 through 10-15* indicate successful routes.

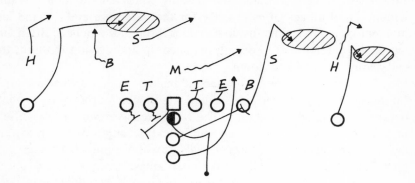

Diagram 10-13

As illustrated in the diagram, the offensive line is aggressive on
the frontside. The quarterback sets back and locates the receiver
with the best passing lane. Linebackers should not be a concern
since they are momentarily held by the fake. Whether the coverage is invert or rotational, either the wide flanker or tight end
should be clear.

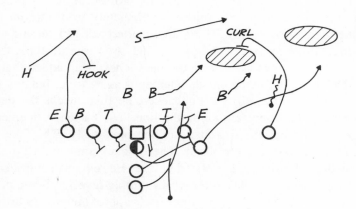

Diagram 10-14

The wide receiver executes the curl with the inside slot darting to
the flat. He has the possibility of swinging deep. Again, whether
the secondary rolls toward the play or not is insignificant. The
linebackers are somewhat geared to the run first before re-
directing to their zones.

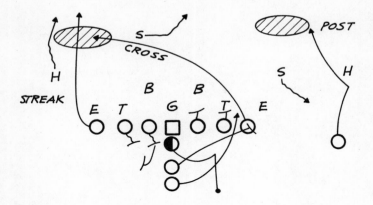

Diagram 10-15

A throwback pass away from rotational coverage can usually discover many open areas. In this case, the backside end streaks downfield to draw the outside cornerback. The right end releases upfield and crosses behind the linebackers approximately 15 to 18 yards. The flanker posts to force the deep safety in the middle zone. The primary receiver is the tight end, but if any of the deep routes become open, the quarterback should pass deep.

11

THE SPLIT-T OPTION

The Split-T option is considered one of the first option series introduced in football. As denoted by its name, splitting along the offensive line is widened to enchance the running abilities of the half-backs.

THE FORMATIONS MOST OFTEN EMPLOYED

The formation adopted with the split-T attack is the straight T formation indicated in *Diagram 11-1*. It was naturally this set that gained tremendous success for the split-T series.

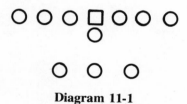

Diagram 11-1

Of course, other formations can be utilized, but when this cocurs the attack is somewhat limited. When the formation varies, however, other strengths become apparent. *Diagrams 11-2 and 11-3* illustrate some of the formations that can be used. Notice that the sets include some form of offensive slot or split end which widens the defense even more for the passing attack.

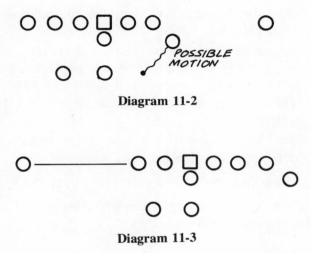

Diagram 11-2

Diagram 11-3

THE STRENGTHS OF THE SPLIT-T ATTACK

The strengths of the split-T sequence of plays are numerous:

1. The offensive line splits force the defense to spread and widen.
2. The width of the offensive line causes a greater area for the defense to pursue to the ball carrier.
3. The series requires quick-hitting plays along the line of scrimmage. A great deal of speed is utilized.
4. There seldom occurs any loss of yardage due to the speed of the plays and the forward momentum of the offensive backs.
5. The offensive backs can break open into the clear more easily and quickly.

6. It is very simple to learn, teach, and understand for the ballplayers.

7. Only a few plays are adopted that attack all areas along the offensive line.

8. Players are interchangeable to either side of the line for learning of assignments in case of injury, personnel changes, etc.

9. Offensive faking occurs along the line rather than in the backfield itself.

10. A great deal of deception occurs with the series, because it is difficult (with the quickness and speed) to determine if it is a straight dive, an option, a counter, or a pass.

11. The best back in his position thrusts at the hole quickly instead of executing delayed timing.

12. Only average personnel is necessary in a number of positions and still makes the series successful.

THEORIES AND PRINCIPLES OF THE SPLIT-T ATTACK

There are four theories or principles involved with the split-T attack. The following are the concepts:

1. Maximum speed
2. Straight ahead thrusts over a broad area
3. Faking at the line of scrimmage
4. Utilization of the "best back" principle

Maximum Speed

The design of this offense is to strike quickly with speed at the line of scrimmage. There is no spinning by the quarterback, deep pitches, or hand-offs in the backfield. The offensive back does not have to attain depth or step forward and then go back from the line of scrimmage.

Straight Ahead Thrusts Over a Broad Area

There are three main objectives for the offensive line to split in order to widen the defense. The most important objective of the entire split-T attack is to utilize intelligent line splits along the line of scrimmage. By widening, the defense must automatically spread. This in turn opens up ready-made holes on the line of scrimmage before the ball is snapped to the quarterback. *Diagram 11-4* illustrates a tight and wide line split. With the utilization of broad splits, the defense has a much wider area to cover than it does with a tight line. Another essential factor is the placement of the offensive backfield. As indicated in *Diagram 11-4,* the offensive backs are also spread with the line. This allows the backs a greater range and wider area of thrust along the line of scrimmage.

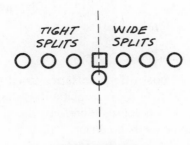

Diagram 11-4

The alignment of three backs located in the backfield presents the offense an excellent and balanced attack to either side of the center. While the three backs give an appearance of a good inside offensive punch, the split-T also presents the offense an opportunity to strike outside quickly and easily.

Another factor with a wide split line is the opportunity to isolate a defender on the line of scrimmage. This is accomplished at the hole or the principal point of attack. With the split, and the isolation of the defender, the offensive back has a better opportunity to break into the clear than ever before. The lineman at the attack point must fire-out quickly at the defender and drive him in either direction. The offensive linemen on either side of the hole must cut-off their defensive counterparts and screen them from the ball carrier.

If the defense doesn't spread and decides to adjust into the gaps created by the splits, the offense can easily block down inside and run or pass outside also. *Diagram 11-5* illustrates a line split and isolation of a defender, while *Diagram 11-6* indicates the blocking angles versus a gap defense (the offense now can attack outside).

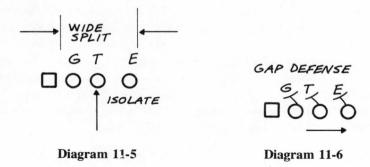

Diagram 11-5   Diagram 11-6

Faking at the Line of Scrimmage

The faking for the most offensive series usually occurs three to four yards in the backfield. In most cases the fake begins at one point deep in the backfield. The defense, therefore, has the opportunity to recover from it and pursue the ball carrier. This is not the case with the split-T series. *Diagram 11-7* clearly indicates the faking areas of the split-T and other attacks.

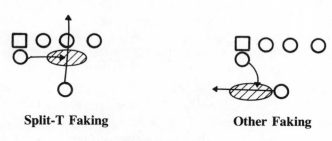

Split-T Faking   Other Faking

Diagram 11-7

Utilization of the Best Back

An essential ingredient of the split-T is getting the best back to the areas of attack quickly. As an example, it is the halfback aligned on either side who can most effectively receive the hand-off from his vantage point. If an offensive halfback from one side of the center must aim at a hole on the other side (presume an off-tackle play), the back has an extended time interval in arriving at the point of attack. With the split-T, this does not occur. The halfback aligned nearest the hole arrives at it quicker. He will either receive the ball from the quarterback or fake into the line. The next ball carrier (in this case the quarterback) continues along the line to the next opening. In this case the split-T is striking quickly with the best offensive back. Emphasized throughout the fundamental split-T series, therefore, is the principle of using the best offensive back to attack the line quickly while establishing a constant backfield maneuver to either side of the center. *Diagram 11-8* shows the basic plays executed from the split-T series.

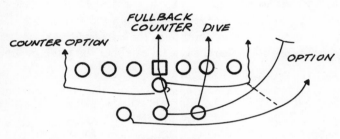

Diagram 11-8

THE SPLIT-T DIVE PLAY

The dive is the first play that should be drilled from the split-T option series. This is illustrated in *Diagram 11-9*. There are a few coaches who practice this as three plays, having the dive drive inside,

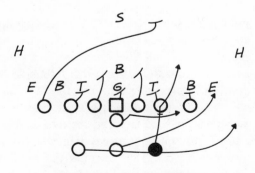

(Versus the 5-3 Defense)

Diagram 11-9

over, and outside the offensive tackle. Each play is designated a number so it can be called versus various defenses. There are other coaches, however, who have the offensive dive back read the defense and break from the blocks of the offensive linemen.

The assignments for the dive play are as follows:

Quarterback

The quarterback receives the ball from the center and steps into the line toward the dive man. The step should never be back and away from the line of scrimmage. The second step follows and should put him into position to present the ball to the dive halfback. He delivers the ball with one hand and continues along the line at the defensive end. He should never gain depth into the backfield. As the defensive end is approached, the quarterback fakes either the pitch or the keep.

Halfback (Ball carrier)

The halfback explodes from his offensive stance and aims straight ahead with all the speed he can muster. As he reaches the line of scrimmage, his eyes focus forward and does not look for the ball. While he is approaching the line, he views the blocking scheme. When he receives the ball, he has the opportunity to swerve either in or out according to the reactions of the defenders. In many cases, the half-back may dart inside where his offside blockers are attempting to assist him.

Fullback

At the snap of the ball, the fullback initiates a crossover step in the direction of the flow and aims for a point two yards in front of the defensive end. He bypasses the defensive end and continues for the halfback as if the play were the option. If executed correctly, the fullback should accelerate at full speed and bowl over the defensive halfback. This serves two purposes: One, the defensive halfback may have a difficult time in determining who has the ball; and two, if the ball carrier swerves outside, the fullback's block may be an important segment of the play. The ball carrier can toss the ball to the trailing halfback and the block thrown may prove helpful.

Trailing Halfback

The halfback immediately starts on a parallel path to the line as if he were to receive the pitch from the quarterback. The halfback, once beyond the defensive end, continues downfield to either block or receive a lateral from the ball carrier.

OFFENSIVE LINE

Blocking along the line is the numbering system (0, 1, 2, 3) explained in detail in Chapter 4. *Diagrams 11-10 through 11-12* illustrate the dive and blocking against the 5-4, Split 4-4, and Pro-4 defenses.

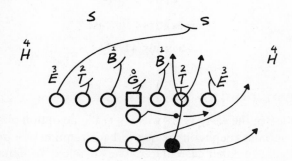

Versus 5-4 Defense

Diagram 11-10

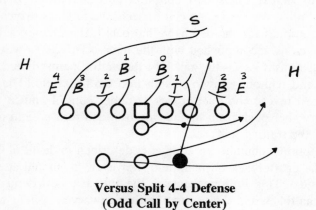

Versus Split 4-4 Defense
(Odd Call by Center)

Diagram 11-11

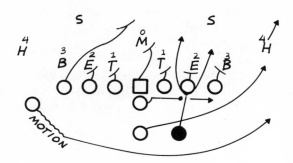

Versus Pro-4 Defense

Diagram 11-12

THE SPLIT-T OPTION PLAY

The option in the early years was not really an option play at all. It was either a definite keep with the quarterback running or a pitch to the trailing halfback. In either case, the fullback blocked the defensive end either inside or out and the play would develop according to the block by him. *Diagrams 11-13 and 11-14* illustrate the toss and the keep, with the fullback blocking the contain man.

As the play progressed, the split-T option, as it is known today, came into existence. The split-T option is illustrated in *Diagram 11-15* versus the Split 4-4 defense. As can be seen, the fullback drives for the end, but continues for the defensive halfback. The quarterback starts along the line as accomplished with the hand-off play. However, the halfback fakes as if he has the ball. The quarterback aims directly at the defensive end without allowing depth into the backfield. The ball is kept at chest level. The quarterback is under control and in a good position to either push from his outside foot and turn upfield or pitch the ball to the trailing halfback.

The option technique, of course, is described in detail in Chapter 2. Once the quarterback turns upfield, however, he should attempt to break outside. This is done because the fullback is driving for the defensive halfback and the trailing halfback swerves upfield with the quarterback even if he does not receive the pitch. *Diagram 11-16* illustrates the quarterback keeping the ball on the option, but then

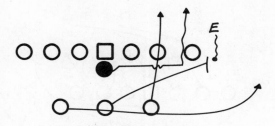

Fullback Blocking Out

Diagram 11-13

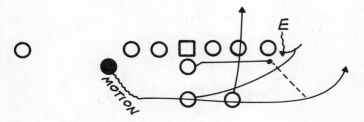

Fullback Blocking In

Diagram 11-14

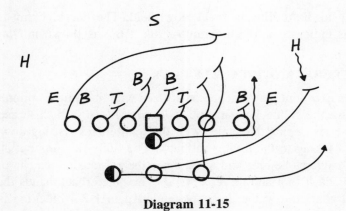

Diagram 11-15

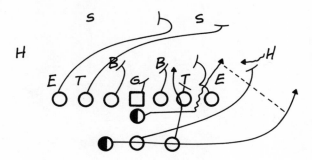

Diagram 11-16

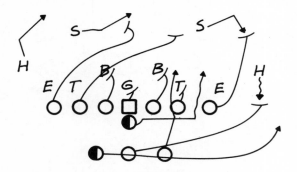

Diagram 11-17

pitching to the trailing halfback downfield. The line blocking is rule "A" as indicated in the diagram or rule "B" as shown in *Diagram 11-17*.

FULLBACK OFF-TACKLE PLAY

An excellent play that can be utilized with the split-T option series is slicing the fullback off-tackle *(Diagram 11-18)*. In this case, the entire series begins the same, with the quarterback darting down the line and faking to the diving halfback. The fullback starts out at a 45 degree angle as before, and as he nears the off-tackle area, he pushes with his back foot and drives upfield. The quarterback hands the ball off and continues at the defensive end. Again 1-2-3 blocking is employed.

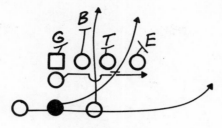

Diagram 11-18

Other blocking maneuvers can be used at the point of attack. Examples include cross-blocks and traps. *Diagram 11-19* indicates the fullback off-tackle play with the onside offensive guard pulling and trapping the defensive end.

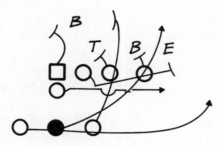

Diagram 11-19

THE QUARTERBACK COUNTER

The quarterback counter is another excellent play from the split-T series. While it may be considered a simple intricate counter without much skill involved, results may prove it is one of the most successful plays of the offense. The quarterback *(Diagram 11-20)* steps along the line as if to hand the ball to the dive back. The strides are short. On the third, he plants and aims back toward the center and glances for the clearing area. While straight ahead blocking can easily be utilized, other schemes such as cross-blocks, folds, and double-teaming can easily be accomplished.

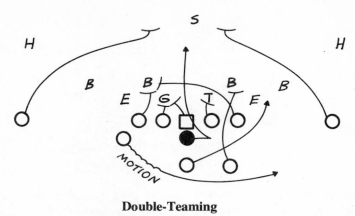

Double-Teaming

Diagram 11-20

THE FULLBACK COUNTER

A major factor of the fullback counter is the pursuit of the defensive team *(Diagram 11-21)*. Since the split-T strikes quick along the line of scrimmage, the defense pursues fast to the ball carrier. Counter plays, therefore, are excellent to decelerate this pursuit. As indicated in the diagram, the fullback initiates a lead-step in the direction of the faking option. However, he pushes off one foot and aims for the opposite—or in this case, the left leg of the offensive center. He accelerates and scans for daylight. Straight-ahead blocking can easily be adapted; however, other blocking schemes can be used with a great deal of success. The quarterback begins his first and second step, pivots back toward the fullback, and hands the ball to him. The diving halfback does all the faking into the line. It is essential the quarterback remains near the line and not gain depth as he spins back to the fullback.

THE SPLIT-T COUNTER OPTION

Diagram 11-22 illustrates a counter option away from the original flow of the backfield. This serves as a form of counter if the defensive team is pursuing well to the front-side attack. The blocking on the line of scrimmage is straight-ahead (Blocking rule B—Chapter 2) with one-on-one blocking. The onside offensive linemen must sustain their blocks due to the delayed actions in the backfield. The quarterback

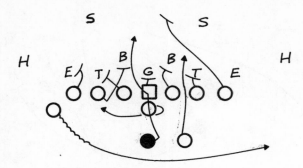

Fold Blocking Against 5-4

Diagram 11-21

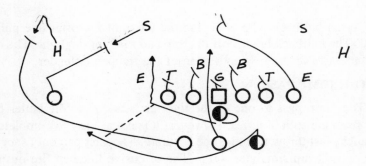

Diagram 11-22

uses identical techniques as in the counter play, but continues along the line for the opposite defensive end. The fullback fakes well up the middle to freeze as many defensive linemen and linebackers as possible. In this case, the left halfback adopts the same rule as the fullback does with the normal split-T option. The right halfback executes a quick jab as if to dive, but reverses his course and becomes the trailing halfback for the pitch. The quarterback utilizes identical option techniques and coaching points at the defensive end as he did with the normal option play.

THE SPLIT-T INSIDE TRAP

Diagram 11-13 indicates a simple trap used with success. The entire backfield starts in the same direction, but the quarterback hands

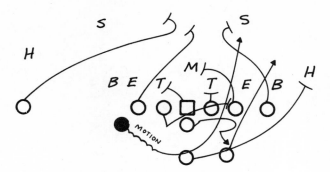

Halfback Inside Trap

Diagram 11-23

back to the halfback who is keying the block of the offensive pulling guard. The halfback breaks off the trap and runs for daylight. The dive back attempts to draw the attention of the trapped defender.

THE JUMP PASS

The jump pass to one of the tight ends is one of the better pass plays from the split-T series. However, it is not as easy to complete. It is a quick, fast throw that must be accurate. The pass can only succeed if the entire team simulates a run. The offensive linemen fire-out low and quickly at their defensive opponents, but should not release downfield. The diving halfback fakes as if he has the football. An essential ingredient of the jump pass is for the diving halfback, once he has reached the line of scrimmage, to aim toward the linebacker or linebackers who can interfere with the pass. If he bluffs a fake in the line, the linebackers will react to him.

The offensive end is a vital factor in the success of the play. His route will alter according to the alignment and reactions of the defensive linebacker. If the linebacker is aligned inside, the end accelerates outside on him. If the linebacker is outside, the end drives inside *(Diagram 11-24)*.

The quarterback's action is important also. He hastens along the line as previously mentioned, but stops short of the diving halfback. He does not go beyond this point because he can be dumped by the defenders outside the offensive tackle. In Diagram 11-24 the proper

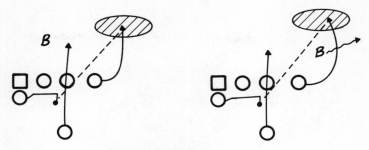

Diagram 11-24

positioning is vividly shown. *Diagram 11-25* illustrates the entire play. Notice the left end releases inside and attempts to block the middle one-third or the defensive safety. Once the right end grabs the ball, he scans inside and swerves from this block.

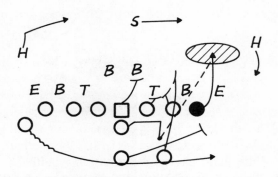

Diagram 11-25

A throwback jump pass can be executed by the quarterback as shown in *Diagram 11-27* also. The quarterback maneuvers down the line, stops and throws back to the opposite end. The pass route is determined, again, by the positions of the linebackers and defensive secondary.

THE RUNNING HALFBACK PASS

Essential to the halfback pass is the offensive linemen's fire-out block and entire backfield fake. It must simulate the run. The quarter-

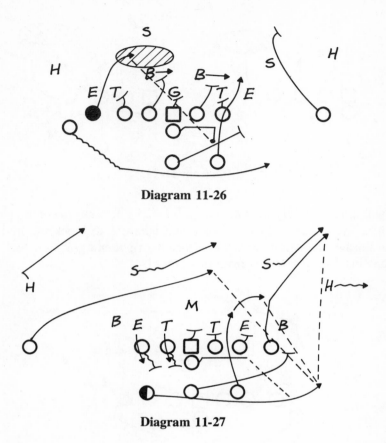

Diagram 11-26

Diagram 11-27

back drives straight down the line and executes a definite delivery to
the halfback. The fullback collapses the defensive end inside. The
halfback grasps the ball and sets to pass. Any number of pass routes
can be utilized with this play. It is important, however, that the halfback be a good passer. This can be drilled enough so the halfback
becomes very proficient at it. *Diagram 11-27* illustrates the running
halfback pass. The passer can either strike his offensive end, halfback,
or opposite tight end.

12

OPTIONS FROM VARIOUS SERIES

An option play can usually be adapted for any offensive series. This is quite apparent with the number of options explained throughout the previous chapters. Other sequences that install the option play as well include the isolation series, cross-buck series, quick pitch series, etc.

THE ISOLATION SERIES

The isolation play means literally just that, i.e., to "isolate" a linebacker in the defensive scheme. An offensive back is responsible for the linebacker. The ball carrier breaks in either direction from his block. The blocking combinations usually alter according to the defensive alignments. The explanation of the isolation and its option follows. *Diagram 12-1* illustrates the isolation with an example of a blocking scheme versus the 5-4 Defense.

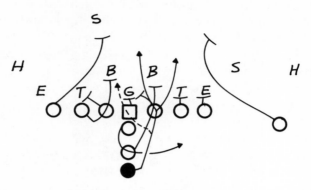

The Isolation Play
Diagram 12-1

The Quarterback

At the start of the play, the quarterback begins to reverse pivot. The first action step is swung back and away from the line and planted directly behind his original stance. The ball is snapped, brought to waist level, and held next to the belt buckle. The second step is shorter and completed parallel to the line (the feet are now aimed toward the sideline). The shoulders are perpendicular to the line with the quarterback prepared to present the ball to the tailback. Once the ball is given and the ball carrier has darted past him, the quarterback continues at the defensive end and fakes the option play.

The Fullback

The fullback sets directly behind the quarterback with his heels approximately four-and-a-half yards from the line. At the snap, he lead-steps bearing toward the first linebacker on the playside. He darts at full speed, leaning forward and remaining low in his thrust. As he approaches the linebacker, he explodes with his shoulder through the outside hip of the defender. His leg drive continues to accelerate once contact is made. His back, hips, and shoulders work up and through the defender which creates proper blocking drive. It also prevents the blocker from stumbling and causing the disruption of the play.

The Tailback

The initial step of the tailback can be one of three movements.

The most common start is for the tailback to jab toward the side of the play as if beginning to run parallel to the line. He pivots from this step, however, and accelerates toward the line and behind the fullback's course. He can swerve in or out according to the reactions of the defenders. The initial jab allows the quarterback to present the ball deep in the backfield. It also gives the tailback ample range to scan for daylight even to the other side of the center.

A second technique is for the ball carrier to jab straight backwards. He now plunges forward and receives the ball late. He can adjust his course according to the defensive pursuit. A third starting technique is a direct thrust at the designated hole. He lead-steps and aims directly behind the fullback. He still attempts to read defensive reactions. This method strikes at the defense quicker, but isn't quite as effective in breaking his course away from pursuit.

Blocking Schemes

The blocking combinations against defensive schemes can be adjusted and altered to attain success. As an example of this *Diagram 12-2* illustrates three different ways the isolation itself can be blocked versus the Split 4-4 Defense. *Diagram 12-3* indicates similar adjustments versus the 5-4 Defense.

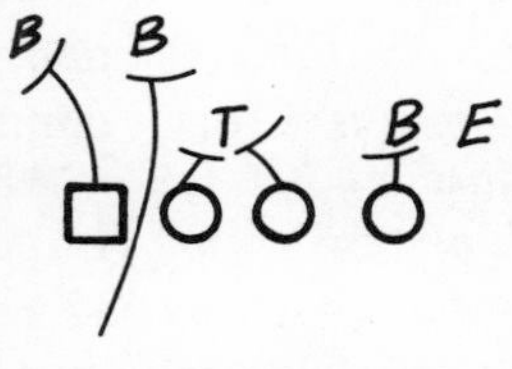

Double Team 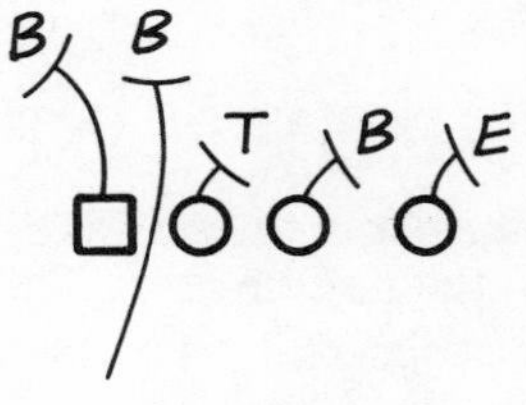   **One on One**

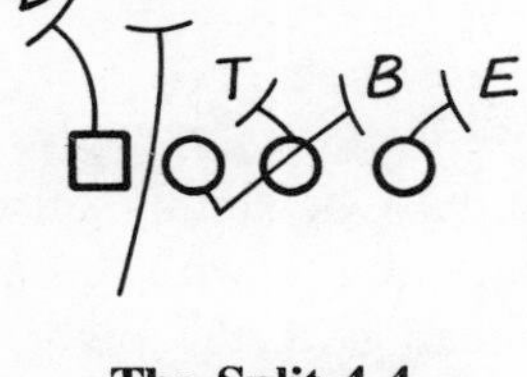

Trap

The Split 4-4

Diagram 12-2

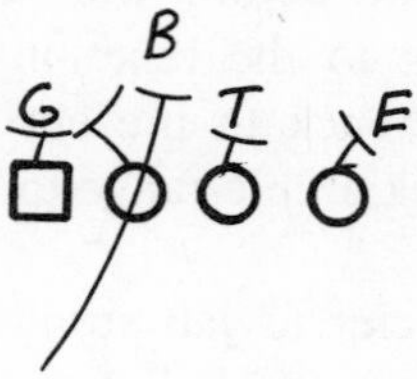

Double Team 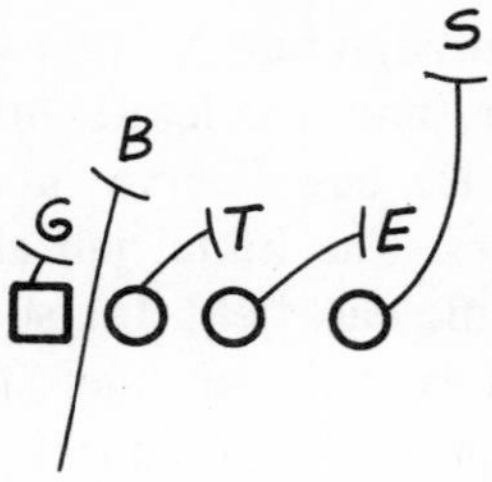   **One on One**

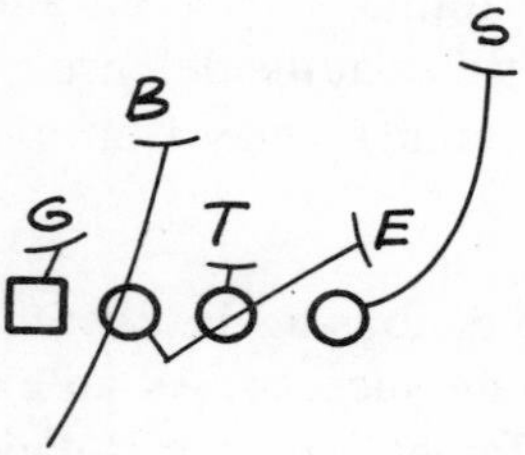

Trap

The 5-4 Defense

Diagram 12-3

THE ISOLATION OPTION

As seen in the isolation play, two backs are driving forward and through the middle area. This sets up the isolation option. If the isolation is successful, the defense will begin to pinch inside. As this occurs, the offense prepares to attack outside. The option now becomes the key to the sequence.

Diagram 12-4 illustrates the isolation option. The backfield techniques change slightly and, of course, the line blocking alters also.

The Quarterback

Instead of the quarterback reverse pivoting with depth as described with the isolation play, he simply spins around nearer the line and presents a fake to the tailback with the hand nearest to the line. While slight depth is gained with the pivot, it is essential that the quarterback attack the defensive end as quickly as possible. As the

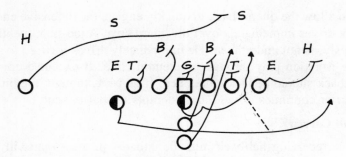

The Isolation Option
Diagram 12-4

tailback darts past him, the quarterback accelerates along the line at the defensive end for the option.

The Fullback

The fullback's assignment modifies according to the blocking scheme installed. If blocking rule "B" is used, the fullback attacks along the same path as the isolation. His assignment is to seal any pursuit reacting outside. If the blocking deviates (an example is *Diagram 12-5*), the fullback aims through the outside hip of the linebacker walling his pursuit outside. The fake of the tailback should support him.

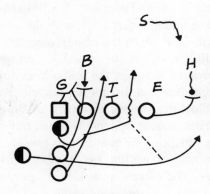

Diagram 12-5

The Tailback

To allow the quarterback to quickly engage the defensive end, the tailback drives immediately over the guard area. A jab step, mentioned previously, is not undertaken. He immediately drives forward to simulate the isolation play through the neutral zone. If executed correctly the tailback should be tackled at once. If he isn't, though, the bluffing ball carrier continues upfield and attempts to seal pursuit.

The Ball Carrier

The receiving halfback must be situated in a set that will place him in an advantageous option-pitch relationship with the quarterback. These alignments include his normal halfback position, slot or wing. From the halfback set he will have to decelerate his pace so he doesn't overrun the quarterback relationship. However, if he starts from the slot or wing, he must accelerate in order to reach the proper position. The fake to the tailback will delay the play long enough for him to arrive at that point.

His stance should be balanced, but with more weight placed on the balls of the feet. At the snap, he pivots on the outside foot and swings the inside foot completely away from the line, aiming on a course that puts him through the normal halfback alignment. A powerful snap of the head and inside arm will assist his impetus backwards and onto his option path.

Blocking Combinations

The standard blocking scheme is the utilization of blocking rule ''B'' described in Chapter 4. Two unique blocking combinations operate quite effectively as well. Diagram 12-5 illustrates a double team against the defensive middle guard (5-4) with the tight end releasing to his assignment in the flat. With the offensive guard slanting down on the defender the linebacker, quite naturally, springs forward for the anticipated ball carrier. This gives the fullback an opportunity to strike a block on the linebacker and disrupt his pursuit outside.

An original blocking scheme is shown in *Diagram 12-6*. Many isolation plays versus various opponents block out on defensive linemen. In the option situation, the guard slants outside toward the defensive tackle, but instead of walling out he slides his head in front to prevent penetration. The offensive tackle scoops outside, but swings

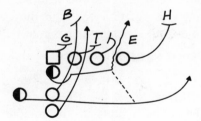

Diagram 12-6

back on the defensive tackle which, as seen, results in a double team block. The end continues to release on his assignment to the corner area and the fullback remains responsible for the linebacker.

The Counter Option

An excellent counter option from the isolation sequence is illustrated in *Diagram 12-7*. The quarterback reverse pivots as he did with the regular isolation option. As the revolution is completed, he hand fakes to the tailback then pushes from his inside foot to retrace the spin. He immediately accelerates along the line to the defensive end. His preparedness to pitch is the key of the play. Once he begins at the end he must be ready to toss the ball, especially if a stunt aims directly toward him. The counter is also a delayed play and possible penetration can be gained along the line.

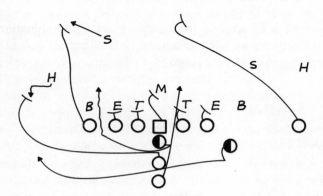

Diagram 12-7

The tailback bolts forward as he did with the regular option. The offside halfback times his relationship with the quarterback for the possible toss. The blocking scheme used is rule "B."

THE CROSS-BUCK SERIES

The cross-buck series can create numerous defensive pursuit problems. Sometimes referred to as the "Delaware" sequence, in the cross-buck series the fullback bolts up the middle with the tailback slanting either off-tackle or circling outside. The quarterback reverse pivots and can either present the ball to the fullback, tailback, or bootleg outside in either direction *(Diagram 12-8)*.

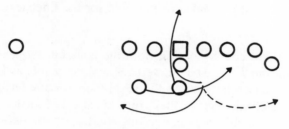

Diagram 12-8

The Fullback

The fullback thrusts forward and reads the defensive reactions from the trap blocker. His aiming point is through the foot of the center to the side of his path. He forms a pocket for the ball and firmly clamps down on the ball as he receives it. He quickly scans the trapper for any clearing. A one-on-one blocking scheme can be used also *(Diagram 12-9)*.

The Off-Tackle Trap

Once the defenders converge toward the fullback dive, the next obvious play is to send the tailback off-tackle. *(Diagram 12-10)*. The quarterback pivots while the fullback passes, introduces his hand as a fake, and reaches to present the ball to the tailback. The quarterback continues with depth in the opposite direction for bootleg action. Trap blocking is used at the point of attack, but other combinations are possible.

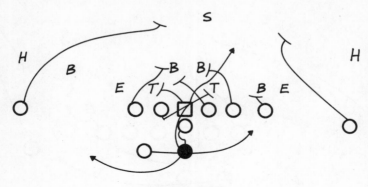

Diagram 12-9

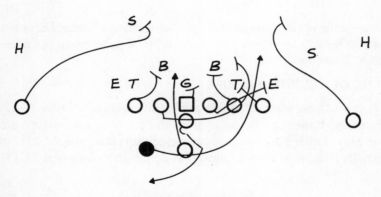

Diagram 12-10

Cross-Buck Option

An option can easily be installed with the crossing sequence. The fullback drives forward and creates a fake to freeze the linebackers. The quarterback reverse pivots which aims him on a course along the line to the defensive end. The tailback scoots on a path parallel to the line and maintains an advantageous option-pitch relationship with the quarterback. Blocking rule "B" described in Chapter 4 is utilized.

The key to the entire play's success lies with the fake of the fullback. The trap itself must gain success through the middle coupled with the fake of the fullback when the option is called. The fullback

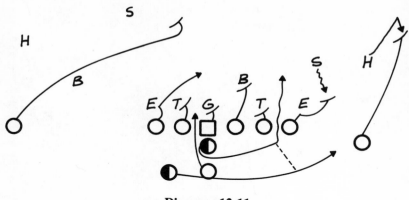

Diagram 12-11

dips toward the option hole in order to slow or freeze linebacker pursuit outside. Offensive line thrust with prevention of penetration is a necessity also *(Diagram 12-11)*.

THE QUICK PITCH SERIES

A few offenses use the quick pitch quite often *(Diagram 12-12)*. Other teams, however sparingly adopt the pitch as a surprise quick outside play. Other plays include an inside trap *(Diagram 12-13)*, off tackle belly *(Diagram 12-14)*, and a play action pass *(Diagram 12-15)*.

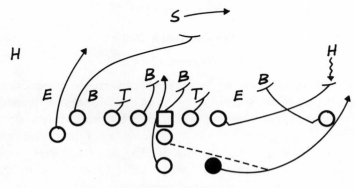

The Quick Pitch

Diagram 12-12

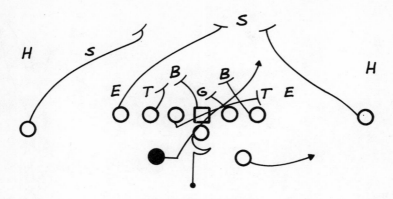

The Inside Trap

Diagram 12-13

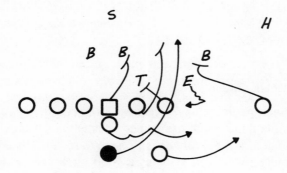

The Off-Tackle Belly

Diagram 12-14

This is an excellent play when the defensive end immediately reacts outside to the quick pitch action. If this occurs, the quarterback simply extends a fake to the tailback and slips the ball into the pocket of the fullback.

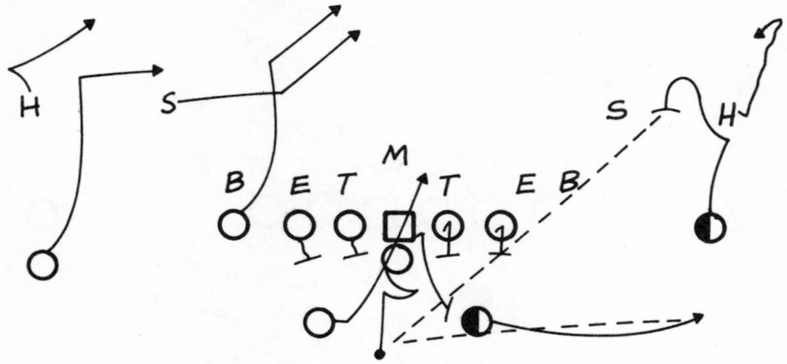

A Play Action Pass

Diagram 12-15

The quarterback simply fakes both to the tailback and halfback trap. He quickly scampers backwards to set for a pass. Any number of routes can be used. An example is the curl pattern as illustrated.

The Quick-Pitch Option

The quick-pitch option *(Diagram 12-16)* coordinates well with the series after the quick-pitch has gained substantial yardage. While motion is indicated, it definitely doesn't have to be introduced. The quarterback simply pivots and initiates a good pitch fake to the tailback. This tends to draw the defensive end outside. The halfback (fullback) dives through the middle to momentarily freeze linebacker pursuit. The quarterback now scoots at the defensive end. If the end widens fast, the quarterback can either keep or pitch the ball according to his reactions. Blocking rule "B" is applied for the quick pitch option.

THE END AS AN OPTION RECEIVER

If an offense has a quick and speedy end, he can be used to attaack as an option receiver. This is an excellent attacking device, as he becomes the "fifth" back. As long as a delayed fake can be completed, the end has the opportunity to swing around into the backfield and arrive in a proper option-pitch relationship. An extra blocker can now be sent in front of the ball carrier. *Diagrams 12-17* and *12-18* illustrate two examples.

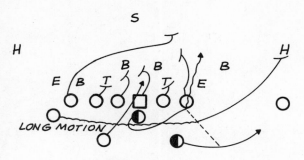

Diagram 12-16

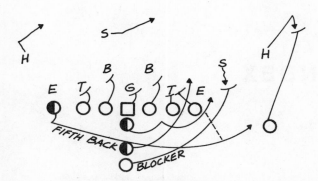

The Outside Belly Option

Diagram 12-17

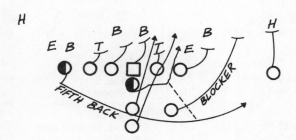

The Isolation Option

Diagram 12-18

INDEX